Expand Your Horizon:

(How to Make Your Faith Work!)

*a **DOVE Christian Book** by Dr. Robert Schuller and Paul Yonggi Cho*

Expand Your Horizon:
(How to Make Your Faith Work!)

by Dr. Robert Schuller and Paul Yonggi Cho

with Dr. Thomas "Tommy" Reid, Bishop John L. Meares, Dr. Samuel Hines
and U.S. Senate Chaplain Richard Halverson

compiled by Florence Biros

DOVE Christian Books
Melbourne, Florida

© 1985, 1988 **National Church Growth Foundation**
ISBN 0-936369-20-5

Cover artwork, graphic design and typography by
Publications Technologies
Eau Gallie, Florida

Printed in the United States of America

Published by
**DOVE Christian Books,
Melbourne, Florida**

and

**SonRise Publishing & Distribution,
New Wilmington, Pa.**

Compiled by Florence Biros
Edited at Publications Technologies

Our gratitude to the founders of the first National Church Growth Conference
and its participants — the dedicated men and women of God who made these
pages possible. We dedicate this book to the Lord Jesus.

The publishers

Contents

Expand Your Horizon: 7

Introduction

Dr. Thomas F. "Tommy" Reid

Prayer can save your marriage!
(But you may have to take out the garbage)

What really pleases my wife, Wanda, is when I take out the garbage. That makes an extreme difference in the happiness of our home since she is embarrassed if I leave early in the morning and she has to drag the trash out to the curb herself in front of all the neighborhood.

When I do this rather demeaning chore, she is greatly honored. It announces to the entire block that I love her and respect her and don't want her out in the street in her housecoat, pleading with the trashman to come back and take one more sack of coffee grinds and orange peels.

God is most interested in that, I discovered in an amazing experience:

I had just begun taking three things with me into my quiet time with the Lord: my Bible, because God speaks to me from His Word; a little notebook called a "Daytimer," in which I write my plans to organize my day; and a larger notebook that I use as a prayer journal.

The Daytimer is important because the most frustrating things in my life are the unprayed prayers, the unmade visits and the parts of my agenda that are left undone. *Why?* Simply because I haven't had time to do them.

Well, as I took all these things into my private meditations with the Creator, I began to have some very strange nudges from the Holy Spirit — not mighty words such as Moses heard when he went into the burning bush — "I AM!" That's not what I heard. What I got when I went down on my knees to pray were such things as, "Tommy, you forgot to take out the garbage!" or — "Did you remember to call Aunt Mary?" and — "By the way, you should have mowed the lawn yesterday."

Now I don't know about you, but that's not the kind of thing that I felt should be going through my mind when I set out to pray.

So I rebuked the devil and tried to turn my thoughts away from such mundane things.

But those fleeting thoughts kept going through my mind "hindering the presence of God" in my opinion. Then — I was hit with the *humbling* thought that perhaps the Holy Spirit was reminding me of God's plan for my home. So the next time I felt the Holy Spirit saying, "Take out the garbage," I wrote it down.

I still do — to this day.

You may chuckle, but when I feel the Lord urging me to take out the trash, I make it part of my plan for the next morning because God has a way of always bringing it to my attention the day before garbage collection!

What I have found is that God talks to me in His mighty and quiet way! God, in my prayer time, can gently organize my entire day!

What am I trying to teach you?

One of the things about prayer is that it is not *just* work.

It's not *merely a holy obligation* that all obedient believers endure as they recite polite observances of God's majesty.

Prayer can be refreshing. Filled with joy. A time when you shut out the world, saying, "I don't want any more interuptions in the next few minutes. Leave me alone and let me pray."

You'll find it exciting as you bare your heart to your Father. Ask Him to help you with your plans for the day. Listen as the Holy Spirit begins reminding you, "Remember to visit Mary in the hospital — Remember to write that letter — Remember ..."

Suddenly prayer takes on an exciting dimension — and it's no longer a dreaded time when we meekly approach the unseen Mighty One and have Him respond with silence. Instead, we find that our great God is waiting to have personal communion with us! Conversation!

By conversation, I mean two-way communication! *How?*

Let me tell you about my prayer journal. In it are all the requests I am making before God. Under each request and each person I am praying for — I leave a blank space. When I mention something before God, I leave time for Him to speak to me about it.

If I'm praying for my son or a brother in Christ, such as Bishop John Meares in Washington, suddenly, as I pray, God will prompt me to "Write Bishop Meares a letter." I may not know that he's going through a particularly hard time in his life, but maybe just a paragraph saying, "I'm praying for you," may make the difference in John's day. When we pray, we should not just be saying, "I want You to bless so and so, but it is permitting God to speak to us about them — the communion of the Holy Spirit. It is God's utmost desire to talk with us!

Prayer is not a monologue.

Prayer is a *two-way street.*

Faith is believing in the possible!

(But you may have to make your island bigger)

A wise professor once advised me back when I was a young man in seminary:

"When you go up in the pulpit, Bob, don't lay your problems onto people. They've got enough without having yours thrown on top of them. They come to church on Sunday morning, desperate. They need a lift. If you've got problems, if you're upset, share it with the elders, share it with your prayer friends, but when you go up there on Sunday mornings, give them a lift — don't give them another load."

So that's my strategy.

However, I'll ask you to understand as I unload about an experience that really made me angry. Korean pastor Dr. Paul Yonggi Cho — who ministers to the largest church in the world, the half-million-member Central Full Gospel Church in Seoul — has ministered to me many, many times in many, many ways through his writings. His book, *The Fourth Dimension,* is one of the great works of our time. But the last time I was with Dr. Cho in Japan, I became very upset. Now, if you see me on TV, you don't see me angry, do you?

I get angry, but not in front of a camera. I get upset, but not on national TV. There's a reason for that — *I listened to my professor and I just don't lose my cool in the pulpit.*

But as Cho and I were driving from Norita Airport into Tokyo, I saw something that made my blood boil!

Maybe ten years before, I'd been the speaker at a church conference in Tokyo. I think it was right after the book *Your Church Has Great Possibilities,* was published. I was telling these Christian leaders in Japan what fantastic possibilities they had for the church, for the church has the most exciting message, if we rightly understand the Gospel of God's grace in Christ Jesus — the most up-to-date message I can think of.

I told them, "You've got to think bigger."

Their defense was that in Tokyo there's a terrible scarcity of land. Churches just can't grow because there's no room for bigger auditoriums and Sunday school complexes.

"Absurd!" I had responded "You never surrender leadership to property! The shoe doesn't tell the foot how big to get!"

"But, Dr. Schuller," they had protested, "if you can seat only 30 people and can't park a single car, how can you possibly grow?"

"For starters," I had answered, "you can have five or six services, then seven services a day. If you seat only 30 people, you still have 210, right? But that's still thinking too small! You've got to make your thinking big enough for God to fit in."

But the Christian leaders argued, "Oh, Dr. Schuller, you don't know what you're talking about. You can't think about bigger churches and bigger buildings. Not in Japan, because Japan is an island. When you're an island, you can't get any bigger. Real estate is pretty scarce and you just can't get any bigger pieces of property to build bigger churches."

Then I told them, "My great-great grandfather was a Dutch baron in the Netherlands. He was instrumental in building dikes. I learned one thing from history: if you live on an island or you own property that touches the ocean, you can enlarge your land base without going to war. All you have to do is push the water back. Go out there a mile into the ocean or half a mile or a quarter of a mile and sink a dam. Then suck the water out and you've got land! Right? Smooth over the dirt and build on it!"

They laughed at me! They mocked me. Boy, did they make fun of me! "Schuller says, 'Push out the water. Make the island bigger. Ho, ho, ho, ho!' "

Their scorn even reached my own denominational head-quarters in New York City. We have missionaries in Japan and, boy, did they make fun of me. I was literally a laughing-stock.

Well, as Cho and I were driving downtown to Tokyo ten years later, I became really angry.

I saw their new Tokyo Disneyland — *built on an artificial island in the middle of Tokyo Bay.*

Disney did what I'd advocated ten years before. *They went into Tokyo Bay.* They filled it in. They put $400 million into it and they opened a park. *They made the island bigger.*

Now, why did that anger me? **I think you know!**

The world was willing to think in terms of possibilities — while the church closed its eyes and just accepted the sad, depressing, terrible reality of what it had decided *had to be!*

That's exactly *backwards* of how things should be!

You know, everybody has under his shirt a red button, a green button and a yellow button. If you want to know how to communicate, you've got to know whom you're talking to. You've got to know what his red button is. Don't you push his red button — it makes him stop listening. He's got a green button, too. That turns him on.

So, find out what his green button is.

But remember, he's got a yellow button also. It tells him: *CAUTION.* Push it and he's going to be suspicious of you.

I'll tell you my red button. My red button is pushed when I see the secular world thinking bigger and demonstrating more courage and daring than the church of Jesus Christ.

That really is my red button.

I'd had to speak to those leaders in Japan and somehow push their green buttons — and somehow not let them know that they'd pushed my red button.

I didn't know what it would take, however.

So, I had opened the Scriptures. So help me, I didn't plan it, the Lord did. This was the passage I read before me — Isaiah 59: 1-2: *"Behold, the Lord's hand is not shortened that it cannot save. Or His ear dulled that it cannot hear. But your iniquities have made a separation between you and your God and your sins have hid His face from you so that He does not hear."*

Did you hear that? Sin! Your iniquities have made a separation between you and your God!

I said to those Christian leaders in Japan — and I throw the same challenge out to you:

"What's the difference between Japan and South Korea? I mean, look at the souls that are being saved in South Korea. Some of the world's biggest congregations are in Korea! Dr. Cho's congregation alone is hoping and praying to hit the 1 million membership mark. But this is not happening in Japan. What's the difference? *Behold, the Lord's hand is not shorter in Japan than it is in Korea.* It's the same length!"

You can look at some of the enormous churches in the United States or in South America that are great witnesses to His majesty. God's arm is not any longer in these churches than it is in the churches that are not growing!

His ear is not dulled that it cannot hear. What is the explanation? That our sins have made a separation between ourselves and our God. Our sins have hid His face. *Now, what does that mean?*

As I read this Scripture that the Lord had spread before me, I prayed swiftly, in a panic, that His Holy Spirit would allow me to interpret it correctly, because I felt that it might be rather insulting to these Japanese believers — who were, of course, blind to their own sin and disbelief.

Should I tell them: *"Your sins have separated you from God"?* What did that mean for them? *Your sins?* Wow! Their churches weren't growing. You didn't see the Lord saving people. Did I dare accuse them of sin?

Why were the lost not being brought to Jesus? *Sin and iniquity.* But what wickedness was rife in these struggling little congregations? Just by looking at these pastors, elders, and deacons in these dead little churches, I knew that none of them were out running around with prostitutes.

I didn't think any were stealing.

Or telling a lot of lies.

I didn't think any were vicious and mean and raping and killing. They were good people. ***Good people!***

They were not a bunch of sinners in the terms of adultery and fornication and theft and all that.

Then what was their sin? Disbelief! What was their iniquity? *A lack of faith.*

I have come to the conclusion that the church isn't going to grow until we come to understand what **sin** is at its core. We're all hung up with this thing that sin is only lying, stealing, killing. Anybody with half a brain knows that's sin. But we don't dare to get to the core of sin: lack of faith.

When you say, "Make the island bigger? That's impossible!" you are waving your lack of faith in God's face!

In that sense, I truly believe we are conceived and born without any faith in God or in ourselves or in anything. The first stage of human development is the first two years of a child's life, where the child learns nothing but trust. The newborn infant is afraid, which is a way of saying he's non-trusting, which is a way of saying we're born in a condition of lack of faith.

I submit that the core of our sin is lack of faith — particularly when we profess to believe.

How do I prove such a stand? Consider Hebrews 11:6:

"Without faith, *it is impossible to please God."* Or we can go to Romans: *"By grace are we saved, through faith."* (That's not of yourself, it's a gift of God.)

We're all hung up, you know, on this doctrine of sin.

So, maybe it's time that we talked about it.

What is sin, anyway?

And how does it show its face in the lifestyle of a defeated believer?

Shall we talk about this problem "sin"?

(No, I don't believe that you are perfect!)

We're never going to have personal and spiritual growth until we recognize that when we confess our sins, we have to confess our lack of faith.

I see it in the doctrine of repentance.

There are people who say, "Schuller never preaches repentance." What they mean is that I do not preach a self-mortifying, a self-flagellating, self-condemning theology, because I think that's purely negative concept of repentance. I think positive repentance is a commitment to faith.

You know I don't use the word *impossible* very often, but I want to say something. I want to say that it is impossible, *impossible,* to come into the presence of Jesus Christ without feeling unclean. I think the most positive way of preaching repentance without taking the risk of doing psychological damage to people who already have a negative self-image, is to lift up Christ and bring them close to Jesus.

I don't think it is possible for people to get close to Christ without feeling a sense of conviction. I feel that the problem is not to make them feel a conviction of guilt, but to get them to believe they can be saved by grace.

Totally by grace.

I must help them to believe in non-judgmental, unconditional, unselective *love* for us by God, the pure and holy Father. That's the most difficult thing in the world to believe.

Repentance isn't just creating — artificially through human manipulation — a tremendous guilt trip. Positive repentance is leading persons into a personal relationship with Jesus until they know Him and He knows them and they have a relationship. In the process, they see His scars and they really come to be accepted as they are.

They know they are forgiven, really forgiven — totally — completely, as in the story is of a girl who claimed she had visitations from the Virgin Mary and that she encountered Jesus and talked to Him. It reached a priest and he investigated. It sounded pretty authentic.

Crowds gathered about her. Then it reached the ears of the archbishop. He thought he should interview her. He asked, "Is it true, young lady, that you see the Virgin Mary?"

"*Yes.*"

"And Jesus?"

"*Yes.*"

"Is it true that you claim Jesus talks to you?"

"*Yes.*"

"And He listens to you?"

"*Yes.*"

"Well, my little lady," the archbishop asked, "do you think the Lord will come back and talk to you again?"

"*Oh sure,*" she replied.

"Well, when He does, would you ask Him a question for me, please?"

"*Of course, your Excellency. What can I ask Him?*"

"The next time Jesus talks to you, ask Him, 'What was the last sin that the Archbishop confessed?'

Time passed. He got a call. It was the girl. She came in and said, *"Jesus came to me and talked to me."*

"Did you remember to ask Him the question?"

"Yes."

"I want to make sure you had the right question. What was my question?

She replied, *"I thought you said, 'Ask Him what is the last sin that the Archbishop confessed?'"*

"Oh, did you ask Him?"

"Yes."

"What did He say?"

"He sat there and He thought and thought and He said, 'I can't remember.'"

Exactly!

That's what the Bible promises us!

Doesn't that remind you of Psalm 32:1? *"...who forgives us all our transgressions and remembers them no more"?*

So, what is real repentance?

Real repentance is to introduce people to Jesus. He convicts them of whatever convictions they need. Then He completes, through the Holy Spirit, the act of repentance. It is not complete, nor does it have integrity, until it leads a person to make a commitment to be and to do what God wants him to be and what God wants him to do. Now that's repentance, because that is fulfilling the faith.

The opposite of faith is sin.

Therefore, true repentance is not just begging mercy and being sorry for our sins. Not at all. That's only half of it. The positive, constructive half is, *"Now, O Lord, what do You want me to do? What do You want me to be? I am repentant of my lack of faith. I dare to believe that You can do anything You want to do. I dare to believe that I, with my limitations, can still be a powerful instrument in Your hands with the power of the Holy Spirit. I'm willing to think as big as You want me to think. I'm willing to make a commitment to do, to go, to be, to try, to build whatever You want me to do, to go, to be, to try, and to build."*

To prepare you for that act of repentance, I believe the Holy Spirit gives you God's ideas and they will always be humanly impossible.

Impossible. You'll be asked to step forward when you don't know how you're going to move. You'll be asked to believe that the impossible is *possible.*

You're going to be asked to make a decision to do something that, to your mind, is not only impossible, but is going to create a lot of problems that, to your mind, are insurmountable.

So what is faith? Faith is making the right decision before you try to solve the problems alone and in your human strength. Faith is making a commitment *while it's still impossible.* If you wait until you know how you're going to pull it off before you make the commitment, that's not faith at all. You're not operating in the arena of faith unless you've made a public commitment where you stand a great possibility of an embarrassing failure.

Possibility thinking is nothing more than Biblical faith put into terminology that secular people will listen to. You have to understand what my strategy is. I was saying to Paul Crouch of the Trinity Broadcasting Network the other night, "Paul, I'm trying to understand myself and my ministry compared to lots of these other ministries. Some ministries — well, let's use a bull's eye and other circles. Let's say the bull's eye represents the solid core of God's most committed people."

"The devout. *The mature.* The learned.

"There are churches and ministries made up from that circle and they minister to themselves. That's one ministry.

"Draw a little circle out here and you have Christians

talking to themselves. You have another circle. Finally, as in every area of influence, you reach the outer rim and then those outside the rim. I suppose that I'm trying to station myself at the outer rim and reach those that are outside the rim completely.

"So I've got to use a different language, a different style and a different strategy. But I cannot change the substance to reach those persons."

So when God gives you an idea, it may seem impossible. It will be a challenge to your faith.

Jesus said, *"If anybody would be my disciple, let him deny himself, take up his cross and follow me."* What does that mean?

It means, *"You're not going to be my disciple unless you deny yourself the comfort that comes when you don't live with daring decisions where you run the risk of possible failure."*

This is another way of saying that you have to be willing to deny yourself the privilege of living with safe decisions all the time. You have to deny yourself and start living by faith.

Deny yourself.

Take up your cross.

Any time we get God's idea and make the commitment to do what God wants us to do, inevitably there will be the cross.

Inevitably.

But we have such incredible promises of success.

Success?

What is success in God's eyes?

Let's look into that.

Chapter 3

Dr. Robert Schuller

Faith requires a willingness to TRY

(Knowing you may become a laughingstock!)

There is no success without sacrifice. Self-denial is an act of faith. Bearing the cross is paying the price to build something — a ministry, a church, a mission or something.

But sacrifice is always *constructive.*

It's not self-defeating, as when you say, "Oh, I'm bearing my cross. I'm persecuted for righteousness' sake."

No, instead, to "deny yourself and take up your cross and follow me" means:

Our God never fails. He always wins!

So, obeying Him means winning. It means **thinking big.** Jesus thought big.

I sat next to somebody on the plane the other day and she didn't know who I was, for which I was relieved for a variety of reasons. It gets very old trying to be a celebrity.

She said to me, "What do you do?"

I said, "Guess."

She said, "Give me a clue."

"I happen to work for the most successful enterprise in the world."

"Oh," she said, "you work for Shell Oil."

"No," I said, "guess again."

She guessed, "You're with International Telephone and Telegraph."

"No. I don't want to be demeaning to these noble institutions, but the truth is, the organization I'm with is into territories before Shell Oil or ITT have even learned the language."

"Really?"

"Yes, I'm very proud. We've been in business longer than both of those corporations put together. "

"I can't figure out what it is. Give me another clue."

"Well, I'll tell you what. We are just about to tap every market in the world."

"You're a marketing man?"

"In a way, you might say that ..."

Finally, of course, I had to give her an answer. "I'm with the church of Jesus Christ."

But everything that I'd told her was absolutely true! I mean, we get into the jungles before anyone else gets there. There are over a billion Christians in the world today and we're growing. I'm following a winner — not a loser. Jesus rose again on Easter. I believe that with all my heart and soul!

I just finished writing an essay for an English publisher on what I believe. They picked 20 people to contribute to a book. I don't know why they picked me, because most of those picked are dead — whatever that says about me!

They picked Einstein and all these big wheels — and then they picked me. At any rate, I wrote, "I believe in God first of all." I believe in God for a variety of reasons — most of all because of my love and devotion to Jesus.

Somebody said to me the other day, "Do you believe in

hell?" I said, "I sure do, because I believe in heaven. If there is no hell, then heaven would be a hell of a place." Just think it through. That's true. It's true. I wouldn't want to go there. Maybe get stuck with Hitler for a roommate for a thousand years. No way.

I believe that Jesus died on the cross to save us of our sins. I believe that He rose again. I believe in the literal, actual resurrection of Jesus Christ.

I had a taxi ride the other day in Honolulu. Oh, I tell you, taxi drivers are a breed apart. God made men, women, children and taxi drivers.

At any rate, this taxi driver was something else. My wife, my daughter and I were together in the cab. He talked from the time he picked us up until the time he dropped us off at the hotel — non-stop. I mean non-stop.

I had his whole life story. Born and raised on an Indian reservation in America. Never learned to read or write. When he was 13 years of age, his parents kicked him out. He heard there was good hunting in the marshes of Honolulu, so he went to Honolulu. He hunted ducks and sold them. That's how he made a living. But he said, "I'm 68 years old now and I've gone through the first grade. I'm still at it and I hope that in two or three years I'll pass the second-grade level."

Then he said, "If I had to do my life over, you know what I'd be?"

I said, "No." But before he got into that, I asked, "But, then you can't read?"

"No."

Do you ever watch TV?"

"No. There's never anything good on TV."

I remained discreetly silent. Then he said, "Do you know what I'd do if I had to live my life over?"

I answered, "No. What?"

"I'd be a preacher."

"Really? Why?"

"These preachers, they make millions of bucks. But you know I'm really happy with my life. I never married, so I don't have any kids to support. All the hookers are friends of mine. So I've got all I want and I don't have any responsibility. Everybody else is jealous of me."

Then he went into another tirade about preachers and churches.

"Are you against churches?" I asked.

"No, churches are good. They're good for people who are bad, but I don't need them. I'd sure like to meet God someday, though."

"Do you believe in God?"

"Oh, yes, I do. I'd like to meet Him someday to ask Him one question."

"What's that?" I asked.

"I'd like to ask Him why in the world He put human beings on Planet Earth anyway."

"Oh? He's already answered that question," I told him.

"He has? When? Where?"

"In the Bible."

"Oh, I've never read the Bible. Can't read."

"Nobody ever read it to you?"

"No."

"Well, in the Bible there's the answer."

He asked, "What is it?"

"Well, God was lonely and He wanted a lot of companionship, so He created the kind of creatures that could think His thoughts and love with His heart the way He loves and be happy and live in joy. He sent Jesus into the world to save us from our sins. You're not perfect, are you?"

"No."

"OK, that means you're a sinner like everybody else. Join the human race. Jesus came to save us."

"He did?" he said. "I didn't know anything about it."

"Well, after dying on the cross to save us of our sins, He rose again. Then He sent his Holy Spirit into the lives of people like me or you — if you want Him to come in. Then Jesus can live inside as He does today. He lives in the bodies of tens of millions of people all over the world and He speaks in every language, has every color of skin, dress syle and culture."

That's what I believe.

I submit that this is just a part of what the Gospel of Jesus Christ is all about. The fundamental attitude for spiritual growth is that we have to repent of our sins and that is repent of not having bigger faith.

A friend of mine once said, "You know what hell would be for me? Hell would be that when I stood before God, He told me all the things I could have done if I'd only had more faith."

"Repentance of sin."

What does it mean?

It means, "I'm willing to be a public failure.

"A laughingstock if that's what You want me to be."

But the Lord would rather that we have the faith to attempt to do something great that He puts in our heart — something great in obedience ... even if we fail.

Rather than attempt to do nothing.

And succeed at it.

Chapter 4

Repent!
(Who ... Me?)

Isaiah 55:6 says: *"Seek the Lord while he may be found, call upon Him while He is near."*

That's an interesting admonition! Isaiah goes on to warn in verse 7: *"Let the wicked forsake his way and the unrighteous man his thoughts; let him return to the Lord, that he may have mercy on him, and to our God, for he will abundantly pardon."*

Now hear this:

"For my thoughts are not your thoughts, neither are your ways my ways, says the Lord. For as the heavens are higher than the earth, so are my ways higher than your ways and my thoughts than your thoughts" Isaiah 55:8 (RSV).

Repentance? Who is to repent? Members of Congress who voted against the Equal Access Bill or school prayer? I can tell you from my own experience personally, as the Chaplain of the Senate, and the experience of many, many members of the Senate that during the two-and-a-half weeks that they voted on the School Prayer Measure, they received thousands of nasty and abusive phone calls from advocates of school prayer. A receptionist in one Senator's office finally went to the Senator, weeping, and said, "I simply can not stand to answer that phone anymore. Please ask someone else to do it."

On a recent news broadcast a woman was being interviewed concerning the Equal Access Bill. The bill was designed to give Christian organizations such as Youth for Christ and the Fellowship of Christian Athletes the same legal access to public facilities as other groups such as 4-H or Future Farmers of America or Young Republicans. She seemed to be a lovely woman, a mother of several children. She described what happened to her and her family when she went to her children's school in California and complained about a religious service there. She was rejected by the community, treated with contempt, threatened over and over and over again and finally, someone burned down her home and left them with nothing except enough insurance to pay the mortgage.

"A servant of the Lord must not be quarrelsome but kindly to every one an apt teacher forbearing, correcting his opponents with gentleness." That's a command from the Holy Spirit or Paul wouldn't have written it!

So, who is supposed to repent? Consider the word itself. In the Greek it means "to reconsider" — "to think differently afterward." Emotions may be involved — sorrow or grief over one's failure or sin — but repentance in the Old and New Testament sense is primarily a rational matter: "I've been thinking wrong about something and I've decided I want to change my way of thinking about that."

Jesus declared, *"I have come not to call the righteous but sinners to repentance."* He said in what is to me one of the amazing texts in the Word of God: *"There is more joy in heaven over one sinner who repents than over 99 just or righteous people who need no repentance."*

I think it's relevant to ask, "Do you give God any joy?" Repentance is a gift of God. God exalted Jesus at His right hand as leader and Savior to give repentance to Israel and forgiveness of sins. Repentance is a gift of God. *"And they glorified God, saying then to the Gentiles also, God has granted repentance to life."*

Paul asked in Romans, *"Do you not know that God's kindness or goodness is meant to lead you to repentance?"* It's not just God's judgment, but His goodness, His patience, His mercy, His grace which are intended to lead to repentance.

There's a passage in II Timothy 2, that is one of my favorites. God gave it to me many years ago in the early days of my pilgrimage with Christ: *"And the Lord's servant must not be quarrelsome."* Do you hear that word from God? In the authorized version it says, *"The Lord's servant must not be quarrelsome, but kindly to every one, an apt teacher, forbearing, correcting his opponents with gentleness."* (2:24-25). God may perhaps grant that they will repent and come to know the truth and they may escape from the snares of the devil after being captured by Him to do His will.

The Lord wants all to come to repentance. The Lord is not slow concerning His promise (as some count slowness), but is forbearing toward you — not wishing that any should perish, but that all should reach repentance.

Godly grief leads to repentance for Godly grief produces repentance that leads to salvation and brings no regret, but worldly grief produces death.

Repentance involves works — or fruit. Luke, chapter 3, says, John the Baptist said, *"to the multitudes that came out to be baptized by him, 'You brood of vipers! Who warned you to flee from the wrath to come? Bear fruits that befit repentance, and do not begin to say to yourselves, I have been a Presbyterian'"* (I beg your pardon — that's not what he said). He said, *"Do you begin to say to yourselves that I have Abraham as my father? For I tell you, God is able from these stones to raise up children to Abraham."*

(He can also raise up Presbyterians from stones — matter of fact — many Presbyterians are stones!) *"Even now the axe is laid to the root of the trees; every tree therefore that does not bear good fruit is cut down and thrown into the fire."* (Remember he is talking about repentance.) *"And the multitudes asked him, 'What then shall we do?'"*

He answered them, *"He who has two coats, let him share with him who has none."* Now, wait a minute, Lord! How about this? It doesn't have anything to do with repentance, does it? *"He who has food, let him do likewise."* Then it says that tax collectors came to Him to be baptized and said to Him, *"Teacher, what shall we do?"* He told them, *"Collect no more than is appointed you."* Soldiers also asked Him — *"And we, what shall we do?"* He said to them, *"Rob no one by violence or by false accusation, and be content with your wages."* What in the world does being content with your wages have to do with repentance?

Paul, testifying before King Agrippa, spoke thusly: *"Wherefore, O King Agrippa, I was not disobedient to the heavenly vision, but declared first to those at Damascus, then at Jerusalem and throughout all the country of Judea, and also to the Gentiles, that they should repent and turn to God and perform deeds worthy of their repentance."* (Acts 26:20,21 RSV).

God brought some vital issues to my mind when I prayed concerning repentance. Many of us are concerned about church growth which has become an exact science in America. It is sometimes treated that way. Someone — I wish I could give you the source, but I can't — said: *"Our faith began in Palestine as an experience; it went to Rome and became an institution; it went to Europe and became a culture; and it came to the United States and became an industry — or an enterprise."*

"Church" is big business in America today!

What is the first thing that comes to your mind when you hear the words, "Church Growth"? Numbers? Size? Quantity? Our culture has made the "big" church a kind of model with the assumption that if you're really a good pastor someday you'll be right "up there." Number, size, quantity (which are really not bad or wrong), are these the proper criteria to judge by?

We desire that all be saved and the greater the number that come to Christ — the greater our joy. We're not sad when lots of people get saved — we praise God for numbers in that respect —and we thank God for the ministries that He's raised up to reach the masses. But the question is, "Is the primary goal of church growth numbers ?"

Dr. Cho says it is not so! Read Ephesians 3 and 4. If you really want to know about church growth, you must study Ephesians. Chapter 4 is the heart of Paul's teaching about the church. I call it "Management by Objective" when I talk about it to businessmen.

Paul tells us in verses 8, 11 and 12, that after Christ, *"ascended up on high, he led captivity captive, and gave gifts unto men — some, apostles and some, prophets; some evangelists; and some pastors, and teachers, that those same might equip the saints for the work of ministry, to build up the body of Christ."* Then he gives us His objective — here is what God is talking about when He talks about growth (beginning with 4:13) — Until we all attain to the unity of the faith and of the knowledge of the Son of God to mature manhood, to the measure of the stature of the fullness of Christ. Then he gives us the negative: *"so that we may no longer be children, tossed to and fro and carried about with every wind of doctrine, by the cunning of men, by their craftiness in deceitful wiles. Rather, speaking the truth in love."* Hallelujah!

In the years that I've walked with Jesus Christ, I have observed many who hit people over the head with truth all the time and alienate them and drive them away from truth by using truth like a club. This is characteristic of the growing church — speaking the truth in love. We are to grow up in every way into Him who is the Head — into Christ from whom the whole Body is joined and knit together by every joint with which it is supplied when each part is working properly — which makes bodily growth and builds itself in love. This is growth as Paul talks about it in Ephesians 4. "Growing into Christ," — becoming more and more like Christ.

Notice that when Paul talks about growing spiritually — he doesn't talk about individuals. We grow together! Thank God, my body grew together — all of the organs and parts grew together. There is in medical science a thing called hypertrophy — the excessive development of one of the organs of the body. That's a real problem in medicine and in the church too. We have a lot of hypertrophies in the church!

They don't care how anyone else is growing. They just pride themselves in their own growth and they feel more and more superior. Comparing themselves with all the other members — they're more spiritual, etc. That's hypertrophy — not a blessing or an asset, but a liability and a problem in the body or the Body of Christ. True growth means we all grow together. The theme here is, "Building the Church Today for Tomorrow." That's our theme!

Four verses from Acts 2 tell what the church looked like right after Pentecost. I love this! "*And they devoted themselves to the apostles teaching and fellowship, to the breaking of bread and the prayers. And all who believed were together and had all things in common; and they sold their possessions and goods and distributed them to all; as any had need. And day by day, attending the temple together and breaking bread in their homes, they partook of food with glad and generous hearts, praising God and having favor with all the people*" (Acts 2:42-47,RSV). The very quality of their lives brought them favor everywhere.

The Holy Spirit caused Dr. Luke to attach at the end of that chapter just one more little sentence — almost incidentally — but this is what it says, *"And the Lord added to their number day by day those who were being saved."*

Think about the way the institutional church mobilizes, trains, equips and advertises for evangelism. But here, this Spirit-filled church just loved each other and devoted themselves to the apostles' doctrine and fellowship — the breaking of bread. In prayer they shared everything they possessed with one another and daily attended the temple together and broke bread in their home — praising God and blessing everybody — as a result of which the church increased. Couldn't help it! You feel the sheer effortlessness of numbers when the church is right with God and each other — right with the Holy Spirit.

It's so easy to organize for evangelism and leave the Holy Spirit out of it. Acts 6:7 tells the cause and effect aspect: *"And the word of God increased; and the number of the disciples multiplied greatly in Jerusalem"* (RSV). The Word of God increased and evangelism happened. You begin to see as you read the New Testament that evangelism is something that just happened all the time when everyone was right with God and each other — when the church was in the Word and growing in the Word, maturing in the Word. *"And the Word of God increased; and the number of disciples multiplied greatly in Jerusalem"* (and I like this!) *"and a great many of the priests were obedient to the faith."* (That's pretty good, too!)

In Acts 9:31, Paul — Saul of Tarsus — meets Christ and the persecution stops and we read at almost the end of Acts 9 (31) — *"So the church throughout all Judea and Galilee and Samaria had peace and was built up; and walking in the fear of the Lord and in the comfort of the Holy Spirit it was multiplied."* It just happened!

Then, Acts 16:5 proclaims: *"So the churches were strength-*

ened in the faith, and they increased in numbers daily." Is it possible that we need to repent about the way we think about church growth much of the time — not that we are indifferent to numbers for we want everyone to be saved — but is it possible that we now need to repent, to change our minds, our thinking?

We need to consider the ascendancy of tradition to the exclusion of the Word of God — an issue that's been troubling me for at least 20 years — the ascendancy of tradition to the exclusion of the Word of God. That's what happened between what I read in Acts and the middle centuries. It's no longer the Word of God, but tradition.

From Mark 7:1-9 Now when the Pharisees gathered with him, with some of the scribes, who had come from Jerusalem, they saw that some of his disciples ate with hands defiled, that is, unwashed. The Pharisees and all the Jews do not eat unless they wash their hands — observing the tradition of the elders when they come from the marketplace, they do not eat unless they purify themselves and there are many other traditions which they observe — the washing of cups and pots and vessels of bronze. Look at what had become important in their religion — and these are the Pharisees — the Fundamentalists! "And the Pharisees and scribes asked him, 'Why do your disciples not live according to the tradition of the elders but eat with hands defiled?' " Now that is really something to be concerned about! Just think of it — here were these proud, brilliant religious leaders whose big concern was eating with unclean hands! We can really get preoccupied with trivia!

And Jesus said to them, "Well did Isaiah prophesy of you hypocrites, as it is written, 'This people honors me with their lips, but their heart is far from me; in vain do they worship me, teaching as doctrines the precepts of me, You leave the commandment of God, and hold fast the tradition of men.' " He then said to them (and here's some beautiful sarcasm!), "You have a fine way of rejecting the commandment of God, in order to keep your tradition!

How much have we allowed evangelical tradition to replace God's truth in our thinking and practices? How often do we make an issue of our traditions instead of the truth? The president of my seminary used to say, when I was in school, "Whatever you make the issue — you make the idol." We evangelicals create a lot of idols — we call them "issues." Is it possible that we need to repent about the substitution of this growing tradition for the Word of God?

There's something else to reconsider — the peril in prosperity. You might not like me for this! In Deuteronomy 8:11, Israel is ready to enter the Promised Land. Moses will not lead them because of disobedience. He is only going to see the land, but he is preparing the people of Israel to enter. This is what he says to them (I'm going abridged): "Take heed lest you forget the Lord your God, ... lest when you have eaten and are full, and have built goodly houses and live in them, and when your herds and flocks multiply, and your silver and gold is multiplied, and all that you have is multiplied, then your heart be lifted up, and you forget the Lord your God."

Thirty-five hundred years ago Moses understood the peril in prosperity. How easily prosperity can replace God! It says further, "Beware lest you say in your heart, 'My power and the might of my hand have gotten me this wealth.' " (That's America! We have really done it!) "You shall remember the Lord your God, for it is He that gives you power to get wealth. And if you forget the Lord your God and go after other gods and serve them and worship them, I solemnly warn you this day that you shall surely perish!" (Deuteronomy 8:17-19 RSV).

God is talking through Moses to the people that He has delivered from bondage in Egypt: "Like the nations that the

Lord makes to perish before you, so shall you perish, because you would not obey the voice of the Lord your God" (18:20).

Revelation 3:14-16 says, "And to the angel of the church in Laodicea write: the words of the Amen, the faithful and true witness, the beginning of God's creation. I know your works: you are neither cold nor hot ... so, because you are lukewarm, and neither cold nor hot, I will spew you out of my mouth.' " (I know it's vulgar, but I always want to say "puke.")

One of my dearest friends was Roger Hall, the former president of Mutual of New York, who is in heaven today. He used to say with great conviction, "The most dangerous man in America today is the casual Christian."

God has told the Israelites about their luke-lukewarmedness, but look at the symptom of this, "For you say I am rich, I have prospered, I need nothing." They needed nothing — not even God.

God assessed them this way, "Not knowing that you are wretched, pitiable, poor, blind, and naked. Therefore I counsel you to buy from me gold refined by fire, that you may be rich, and white garments to clothe you and to keep the shame of your nakedness from being seen, and salve to anoint you eyes, that you may see. Those whom I love, I reprove and chasten; so be zealous and repent." Next comes that beautiful verse spoken to the church. We use it usually with unbelievers, but it was spoken to the church: "Behold, I stand at the door and knock; If anyone hears my voice and opens the door, I will come in to him and eat with him, and he with me" (Revelation 3:17-20 RSV).

Is it possible we need to repent of the fact that we have allowed prosperity to cause us to forget God? I have been bringing this message based upon Deuteronomy 8 and Revelation 3 to governors' and mayors' prayer breakfasts all over this nation for several years. Are we unconsciously —

little by little — misplacing our hope for the future? Please think about this. Jesus said, *"Seek ye first the kingdom of God, and his righteousness; and all these things shall be added unto you."* (Matthew 6:33) He meant that God's kingdom and His righteousness should have priority in our lives — that was to come first! The words "righteousness" and "justice" are synonymous in both Hebrew and Greek. Try translating that as the "kingdom of God and His justice" or "blessed are they that hunger and thirst after justice" — or "I'm not ashamed of the Gospel of Christ because it is the power of God unto salvation for everyone that believes — to the Jew first and also the Greek because therein (that is the gospel) the justice of God is revealed from faith to faith, as it is written the just shall live by faith."

Is God's kingdom and its righteousness — its justice — first in our priorities? I don't know if it is in you. I've examined myself about this — what about you? Are we really kingdom of God people? Is heaven our home or is this world our home — are we like our father Abraham — strangers and sojourners in this life — or have we become very happy and comfortable as citizens here and now?

I was born in Christ in a revival environment way back in 1936 in Los Angeles, California, and spent at least one day a month with 200 or 300 preachers praying for an awakening and also studying the Word of God. We wanted awakening! I can't remember when I didn't long for revival and pray for revival in the years that I've been walking with Jesus Christ.

But I have been amazed sometimes as I have understood people who want revival so that the good old U.S.A. would be saved from the Soviet Union, saved from inflation and recession, saved from depression so we could go on and be more comfortable than ever before. "God, save the good old U.S.A."

I was reading Luke 24 at this year's Easter sunrise service at Redstone Arsenal in Alabama about the familiar story of the two men on the road to Emmaus. I was going to preach on that theme. As I was reading that passage I thought something that I hadn't thought at all as I'd been preparing the message. Do you remember how Jesus came alongside these two men and their eyes were beholden so they did not know it was He? He asked them, "Why are you so sad? What are you talking about?"

They replied, "Are you a stranger — a visitor — that you do not know what has been happening these past three days?" There they rehearsed for Jesus the things that had happened and then three little words came in their explanation, "But we trusted." Those three words hit me in such a way that I could hardly finish the message. I wanted to leave and just consider them. Think what they were saying — they were saying, "We spent three years with Jesus. We saw everything He did, we heard everything He said, we felt His incredible presence, and we really thought He was going to do it! But He didn't! But we trusted — yet He failed us!"

Had Jesus failed? No! But — you see — they had their own idea of what Jesus was supposed to accomplish in the world. You remember when Peter made his great confession and Jesus commended Him? "Flesh and blood is not revealed to thee, but my Father which is in heaven." And then Jesus began to talk to them about His own death in Jerusalem — about His burial and resurrection — and the record says that Peter, who had just made his great confession, recognized Him as the great Messiah. It says that Peter took Him and rebuked Him. Imagine! Peter rebuked the Messiah! He said, "Far be it from thee, Lord!" And Jesus had to say, "Get thee behind me, Satan. Thou savorest not things of God, but of man."

How could they have gotten their Messianic hope so screwed up that they didn't recognize Jesus as the Messiah? He didn't recognize Him as the Messiah because He didn't establish His reign on the earth right then and give the kingdom back to Israel. As a matter of fact, in Acts, the last question they asked before His ascension was, *"Lord, will thou at this time restore the kingdom to Israel?"* Now, let me rephrase that: "Lord, wilt thou at this time — save America?"

Some years ago Malcolm Muggeridge was our guest at Fellowship House, which is at the heart of our prayer breakfast movement, and that morning Muggeridge gave a testimony of what he calls his "Rediscovery of Jesus." It was a wonderful testimony, and then for a few minutes he spoke off the cuff about world affairs. He is always pessimistic when he views world affairs.

When he opened up for some comments or questions, one of our brothers there who simply is incapable of hearing anything pessimistic — he has to hear optimistic things — said: "Brother Muggeridge, you have been very pessimistic. Don't you see anything to be optimistic about?"

Muggeridge answered, "My brother, I am intensely optimistic because I hope only in Jesus Christ and His return!" There was silence as we pondered his statement. And then Muggeridge said this: "Just suppose the Apostolic Church had pinned its hope on the Roman Empire."

There's a familiar text that began to come to the foreground a couple of years before the bicentennial — a text that we felt somehow might call America back to her spiritual roots, and we desperately need to do that. And so, the text from 2 Chronicles 7:14 which begins *"If my people who are called by my name ...."* "Most of it is very clear but some of it is ambiguous. "If my people," — that's clear. *"Who are called by my name,"* — that we understand. *"... shall humble themselves, and pray, and seek my face, and turn from their wicked ways; then will I hear from heaven, and will forgive their sin, and will heal their land."* The wicked ways are the wicked ways that God's people must turn from today!

Is it not possible that the things we have considered here are one way of looking at it — all great and wonderful — yet is it possible that they represent an attachment to this world and this life that betrays a lack of commitment to Christ and His kingdom? These are the wicked things from which we must turn away. It's easy to use that text to think of things like adultery and abortion and robbery and murder. We don't do any of those things so we feel we have no wicked way from which to turn. Is it conceivable that almost all the things we hold so dear — so common to this land in which we live — that are really antithetical to the kingdom of God — is it possible that they are the things from which we must turn away?

I've been absolutely amazed at the surprise with which the evangelicals view the fact that the world is not treating them very friendly today. Talk about humanism and secular humanism — they're bad to us! Well, where do we find in the Bible that we're to expect anything else. Jesus said, "In the world you will have tribulation." Did Jesus not say that? But Jesus also said, "Be of good cheer for I have overcome the world. They hated me, they will hate you." Friendship with the world is enmity with God.

The world put Him on the cross. What in the world should we expect? Why should we expect anything different?

Saturate your life in prayer!

(I did and it changed me — dramatically)

In many of the places around the world they introduce me as a "big shot," but I'm still struggling as a pastor and I often go home after preaching a sermon and beg my wife to preach the next Sunday in my place.

Every Sunday I struggle and am deeply dependent on the Holy Spirit. Without the Holy Spirit, I can never produce any more messages for the following Sunday. Purely because of the work of the Holy Spirit, I found myself pastor of a church of more than a half-million members without ever recognizing the fact that it was reaching such tremendous growth. I am enjoying my pastoral ministry every minute.

To me, prayer is my privilege and my labor.

My whole life is saturated with prayer!

We have a massive prayer program in our church. When I start my Sunday morning service, we have a unison prayer in a loud voice. If I don't ring a bell, my people would stay praying for a whole day, so I have to stop them by ringing the bell several times. We not only pray for our nation, but before I preach I ask my people to pray for the United States of America. We are indebted to America because 100 American missionaries came to Korea one Easter Sunday.

Through their labor we received the light from the Lord and our country became Christian — almost! We now have 10 million professing Christians. Since we feel such gratitude to America, it is our turn to return favors to America. So I ask my people to pray for America. I ask them to pray for the American president, the senators and congressmen and the people in the American church. We all pray for America every Sunday morning and during our Wednesday and Friday all-night prayer meetings.

Our services start with fervent prayer. After the sermon we all pray again to digest the message of the Holy Spirit. Wednesdays, of course, we have Bible study, but our main emphasis is on prayer. We are really saturating ourselves with prayer. On Friday nights we have all-night prayer meetings. Thirteen thousand people come to them in our main sanctuary, and we stay for the whole night and pray. We have praising services, we share testimonies, some short messages about the Bible and then we pray. We stay in the church all night.

At the same time we have Prayer Mountain out in the country. We would rather call it "Prayer City" or "Haven of Prayer." Every day we have 3,000 people who go up there to fast and pray. We call it "Fast and Pray Mountain" because that's what our people do there.

Most of our people are fasting and praying from three to 40 days a year, and so we are well-trained to pray.

Every day we have an early morning prayer meeting. In Seoul I am in charge of all those meetings when I am there. In Korea it gets very cold and it is a hard job to get up at 4:30 and go out to church and conduct an early-morning prayer session. When I come out of my country, I enjoy late morning sleep!

One morning I overslept. I'd worked late into the night, so I slept in. The telephone rang. Still in a groggy condition from my slumber, I heard my mother-in-law rebuking me. She said, "We've been waiting here in the church for 30 minutes, but still you are not appearing. What's happened? Are you still sleeping?"

I looked at my watch and was aghast. It was five o'clock! I was supposed to be at the church at 4:30! I jumped out of bed, dashed into the bathroom and brushed my teeth, grabbed my Bible and rushed off to the church to speak.

People were packing the church. I nearly ran up to the platform, opened my Bible, and noticed they were all rolling and laughing! I looked at myself — I was in my pajamas! Really, in Korea, whether you go out in pajamas or a suit — you should pray!

Many people come to me and ask, "What is your first priority in your ministry?" I answer, "My first priority is prayer." I always pray between one and two hours in the morning. Even in a motel this morning I got up at 3:30 and I've already prayed for one to two hours. Prayer is my second nature. Without praying, I can't start living that day because my heart becomes angry toward myself if I don't pray.

During lunchtime I pray about a half-hour more. In the evening I always pray about one hour. Every day I pray a total of three to four hours. Without such a prayer background, I could never carry out the ministry of my church.

People ask me this question, "Why should you pray so much?" There is a reason for this. I want to share here and open up my heart so that my experience will make your own ministry profitable.

I'm praying because I can only receive the light of the Holy Spirit by repenting genuinely through prayer every day. If I don't pray, I won't really repent because every day I become contaminated by the world of sin. Because we are all living in a sinful world, we are constantly being contaminated. And so, when I pray, the Holy Spirit comes into my heart and I can see my reality and can genuinely repent of my sins.

Of course, every day I commit many sins of the lips because I hear so much from people and then I'm tempted to cooperate with them to criticize others. Even when I pray in the Holy Spirit, He shines up in my heart and rebukes me about some of these situations. I fight the habitual sin of criticizing others. I determine over and over again to completely rid myself of that sin, but again and again I fall into that trap. Therefore I need to get cleansed every day and if I don't pray, I can't get myself cleansed by the blood of Jesus Christ.

I've been in my ministry for 26 years, but still I need the Holy Spirit every day to cleanse my life because there are many temptations that creep in. When you become the pastor of almost a half-million people, you are in the center of temptation. You are in the temptation of making money. If I have the desire, I can make big money, not small pennies, but big money! And legally! It would not be illegal at all. I could become a multi-millionaire! The devil comes to me and says, "Yes, you can become a millionaire legally. Why don't you make money while you have the chance?"

Also, there is tremendous temptation from the opposite sex. You become like an angel to them. On the platform I always talk about the Word of God and they think I'm an angel sent from the Lord. One day my wife came to me and said, "Let's go to the platform and live there together."

I asked, "Why?"

Her answer was simple, "You talk like an angel on the platform, but then when you come home you become a red, hot-blooded human being and I am so confused."

Since I represent Jesus Christ, my people take me as an angel from the Lord — so the temptation from the women is tremendous. I used to think that when I was 50, I'd be exempted from those temptations. When I was in my 20s and 30s I used to pray, "Oh, God, make me an old cat very quickly!" Now I'm beginning to see that temptation is even more subtle at this age. If I don't pray, I can very easily become the target of that temptation.

Also there is the temptation of pride because people treat me like a king. They try to touch me. They swarm around and struggle even to touch my coat. The devil comes and tries to put pride into my heart. If I don't pray, I can't see the real situation of my heart because the devil comes and says, "This is legal and you are justified to be proud." Justified or unjustified, I could really see the reality of the situation only when the Holy Spirit helps me. For this reason, when I pray, the Holy Spirit shines up in my heart and I begin to see myself through the eyes of God and then I repent daily. If I don't go before Him asking forgiveness daily, then I cannot keep my position straight before the Lord. I need to pray so I can be delivered from worldliness because worldliness is strong — like a mighty wave.

To keep myself in Christ's likeness I need to repent. One of Dr. Halverson's messages on repentance hit like a two-edged sword into my heart and I wondered if he had received a special revelation against me!

When I come to my office at 8:30 in the morning, thousands of problems are waiting for me. If I don't check the resources of God through prayer, I cannot meet the daily challenge of my work. I need spiritual resources, I need mental resources, I even need physical resources to depend upon. If I don't have communication long enough with the Holy Spirit, I soon know I have a dry well. In two days my secretary knows, in three days my associates know.

If I don't pray in three days, my whole congregation knows

right away that my well is dried up. To be filled with the resource of heavenly power, I've got to pray.

I was privileged to envision the world's largest church while on my knees.

Even today, if I quit praying, I would slide back to nothingness.

Let me tell you why I believe that.

Chapter 6
Dr. Paul Yonggi Cho

Prayer can take you to the heights
(I was nothing. Without prayer, I still am!)

In 1958 when I first pioneered my work in the suburbs of Seoul, I knew little about prayer life. We were so poor after the Korean War. The economy was in shambles and I was living from hand to mouth. I prayed then — not because I was spiritual — but because I needed an everyday meal from the Lord. I was always fasting and praying, not because of my spirituality, but because I was forced to do so. I had nothing to eat! And so, I really prayed and that became the foundation for the tremendous growth of my ministry. Through prayer I can really stand before the Lord in a righteous way.

In other words, I cannot sustain myself through the anointing of the Holy Spirit. For my own survival I have to pray. I must pray whether people like me or not. Since I was praying so fervently, one by one my disciples began to take after me. Sheep follow after the shepherd. If a leader doesn't pray, people will never follow. You may instruct them to pray, but if you don't practice your prayer life, none will follow you. Since I was so intent on my prayer life, all my associates — my elders and deacons — all began to pray. Because of this our church is wonderfully organized to pray. When I suggest, "Let's pray," they will go into prayer for hours and hours. I have to ring the bell to stop them. It is really beautiful.

I pray because I can break down the opposition of Satan through prayer. Throughout my ministry I have never seen any division in my church! We have a lot of arguments among our ministers and elders. Koreans are much like Latin people. It's as if we had Latin blood. If you have two Koreans, you have three ideas. Because of this, we have a lot of struggles, but through all these struggles, I have never seen any division in my church. That is why we are growing so fast.

Every day Satan visits and tries to create an argument and cause division among my people, but I always bind the power of Satan. "You power of Satan among the elders — I cast you out in the name of Jesus!" We have more than 30,000 deacons. If I don't bind Satan, those 30,000 deacons will have more than 30,000 ideas among themselves. I bind the devils who want to cause disturbance in our ministry and our church.

Paul says, "We are wrestling against principalities and the powers of the air." That's not just theory, that's practical. I have got to fight to bind them. Since I have been binding and praying, we have had many crises, but we have not had any division at all thus far. That's the reason we are growing so fast.

Wherever we go, we meet the strongholds of the enemy — of Satan. Every town has its own devil. If I ever would like to establish a church in a certain area, I have to challenge that power first. If I can defeat the devil, then I can build my church.

When I was first pioneering the church in Seoul, I found a

shrine built to the area devil. They were all worshiping and belonging to the devil. As soon as I tried to establish my church, the priest of the shrine started to challenge. That's all life or death struggle, and without conquering that spirit, you can't free the people. Either you get chased out of town, or you'll get killed. It's very serious there.

In America you are born into a Christian culture so you don't see that kind of situation. In our country they have been in heathenism for more than 4,000 years and they have that spiritual bondage. In 1958 I tried for more than three months, but I could not win one soul to Jesus Christ because those connected with that priest were always following me and intimidating me. They tried to kill me. My main struggle was to see if I could really conquer the devil or would have to move out of the area. I was fervently praying because my work was through prayer.

Then their disciples came to me and challenged me. They said, "If you truly believe you are to be here, we contest you to pray for a lady who has suffered with paralysis for seven years. If your God can do something for her, we will let you have church here. Otherwise you are going to move out of this place, or you are going to be killed!" That was the challenge from the devil!

The whole town was watching me. When I went to see the woman, she was a most miserable situation, for she was the wife of a farmer and alcoholic. She had been paralyzed for years, and in that situation she had given birth to a child. The whole house was so dirty, so smelly. When I tried to tell her about Jesus, she said, "Please, mister, if you can do anything for me, destroy me. If you can do anything, let me die."

I cleaned all the rooms and cleaned the house. I cooked soup and brought it to her — soup I could not even afford myself. I tried everything, but I could not help her. She was completely paralyzed. I became desperate. When I am under pressure, I can pray better. So I fasted and prayed. I really prayed!

One evening I was praying fervently, "Oh, God, help me. If You won't heal that woman, then I should move out of this town." About 10 p.m., I fell into a trance while I was praying. During my prayer I began to hear eerie music and I saw a creature with a snake for a body and the head of a beautiful woman. It was standing on its tail dancing to the music. It came toward me and jumped up on me. I grabbed the neck of the snake as it tried again and again to bite me, and I was trembling. I knew I was losing the battle. That fight lasted for three hours and I was completely soaked with perspiration. The snake came nearer and nearer to me. I could look right into its eyes. I knew it was trying to finish me off.

A voice said in my ear, "Say the name of Jesus." Without saying the name of the Lord, I was struggling in my human strength. I tried to say, "Jesus," but I was so numb with fear that I could not even pronounce His name. In my heart I kept repeating, "Jesus, Jesus, Jesus." Suddenly I could read the fear in the eyes of the snake. Then the power came and I said the precious name, "Jesus!"

The devil slumped down and I crushed it with the heel of my foot. The teeth and the eyes came out. I coiled up the snake and took it to the people for them to see. Satan was conquered!

Then I came out of my trance, but I was completely exhausted. I did not know the meaning of that experience then. But the next morning when I came out of my prayer meeting at my tent church, a big crowd was moving toward the tent. "Oh, oh!" I thought. "They're coming to destroy my church. This is the last of it."

One woman was at the head of the crowd. I looked at the woman and suddenly recognized — she was the woman who was paralyzed! All the others were following her. She was walking toward me carrying her baby. She said, "Thank you, pastor. I really appreciate it that you came to my house at 2 a.m. this morning.

I said, "I did not go to your house at 2 a.m."

She said, "Oh, pastor, you came. I was suffering terribly and you were in our yard. You shouted to me, 'Woman, in the name of Jesus Christ — rise up and walk!' You clearly told me. And so, at 2 a.m. I took up my baby — I could take up my baby! I rose up and was healed! I began to speak in a strange language. I really appreciate you because you loved me so much that you came so early this morning — at 2 a.m. — to announce my healing."

She was completely healed so the whole town followed her. The people chased out the demonic priest and destroyed the shrine. They gave the area to me and I gave it to a missionary and right now there is a beautiful church where the devil's shrine was! That battle was completely won — not by my eloquence, but by prayer.

Before I came out of that town, we had 600 members and a beautiful sanctuary. It was a tremendous victory — won on my knees. From that, I learned that we had to conquer the power in the air before we could establish a church.

You have different kinds of devils in different areas. I can name them, but you know the situation. Pray and fast and destroy the resistance. Otherwise you cannot build a strong church. If you go into an area to bring revival, first fight with Satan who is overpowering the area. When you have conquered Satan, you loose the power to lead souls to Jesus.

I know an American by the name of Curry Vaughan who pastors at Zion Fellowship in Malabar, Florida. He used to be a U.S. Army chaplain in Germany, then he came to Korea to work with the 8th Army in Seoul. He built the largest chapel outside the U.S. He was amazed and came to me and asked, "Pastor, how come my chapel is packed with soldiers every Sunday? They give their hearts to Jesus Christ.

Generals are saved, colonels are saved, privates are saved. I've never seen this sort of thing happen in my life. Matter of fact, I am not preaching any specific message. I am just refeshing the old message I had in Germany. It's as though I brought them canned from there. When I open the can, I refresh and preach the same message.

"In Germany I had some fruit from the message, but here the same message is like a two-edged sword. People are getting saved. How come?"

I said, "Well, Col. Vaughan, in Germany the Christians are not praying, so the power in the air is so powerful that the devil is causing such confusion in the minds of the people that they cannot accept the doctrine of Jesus Christ, but here in Korea, ten million Christians are praying — praying in the early morning on the Prayer Mountain, praying all night on Friday, praying in the cell system. Since we pray so much, the power in the air is broken, and that is the reason the Holy Spirit can really work and the people are not feeling the obsession, the oppression, or even the depression of Satan. They are free from his bondage, and for this reason the Gospel of Jesus is reaching our people."

That is true! Whenever I pray in Korea, it is so easy to lead souls to Jesus Christ. Author C. Peter Wagner planned to come to my church several years ago. I invited him to speak to my people, but he insisted, "I am not a pastor or a preacher, so souls will not be saved under my ministry."

I replied, "Peter, this is a different place. You come and preach. You'll see." Peter came. He was sitting on my right side when the service was going on. I looked at him. He was trembling. I asked, "Peter, are you sick?"

He answered, "I don't know why I am trembling."

But he was trembling and his face was very red. I was afraid he had high blood pressure and was going to have a stroke or something. Right there — sitting at my right side — he was baptized in the Holy Spirit. He stood up and preached like a fiery preacher! I had a hard time interpreting because he was speaking so fast — in such a fervent way. After he completed his message, he asked the sinners to come out. More than 300 stood up to be saved!

He said, "Throughout all my life in my ministry, the total of people I have lead to salvation is less than 300! In one day I have seen more people saved than all the other days combined because I did it without the real anointing before!"

Prayer breaks the power of Satan through the Holy Spirit and it gives us free-working power. For this reason we should pray very hard. When I go to Japan they have eight million gods. When I try to preach the Gospel, I feel so choked. I feel like dying. I hate myself.

In Japan, if there are 50 people in a church, the minister walks like a big shot. Fifty people is a great accomplishment there. In Japan, if you have 500 people turn out for an evangelistic meeting, that is top-notch. Very hard place! To have real victory there, I have to pray for five hours. Without five hours on my knees in my hotel room, I'd better forget preaching. By praying and travailing, I conquer Satan and then I can get through to their hearts. God has given me favor and I always get the largest crowd in Japan. We can only get great crowds in Tokyo through fervent prayer.

When I go to Europe, I always have to pray at least three hours for one sermon because it is also a very difficult place. But when I come to America, I only pray for one hour because you have more of the Holy Spirit than any other place. I feel more free in my heart here than anywhere else.

Just preaching the message will not bring results. Your message should be backed up with powerful prayer. Your life should be saturated with prayer in such a way that you destroy the opposing power of Satan. We are really wrestling in the spiritual realm and before you have victory in the spiritual realm in your closet, you can't have victory in your ministry. For this reason I spend time in my closet on my knees.

Prayer is hard labor. I'd rather do home-visiting, because home-visiting is very interesting. You are talking to people and it is enjoyable. But in your prayer closet, you sit down before God for hours and hours and it is really painful and laborious — especially when I try to go into prayer for 30 minutes because then the devil joins in the fight. I become itchy all over when I pray then! The devil says, "Why don't you quit praying and go out and preach! You're wasting time here!"

For about 30 minutes I fight against my flesh and my itchiness. When I conquer the situation after 30 minutes, then I can barely start flying up and going into the spiritual realm — the Fourth Dimension of the Spirit. At that point I can really pray through. Prayer is a great labor, but to have a victory in ministry, you must pray. House-visiting is far more pleasant, but without prayer you are powerless.

We now have a better church than before — better organized, better educated ministers, but do you know why we don't always have the same impacting power? Because we lack prayer! Without prayer you will not have revival because the devil has the upper hand over you. You will always be the underdog, if after you have preached the Gospel, the devil is still there. If you preach without praying, the devil is very pleased. In the church the devil can rise up and start trouble among your board members and deacons and start some bickering among Christians because the devil wants you to stop your praying. But keep on praying! You will have great victory! For this reason I pray always.

Chapter 7

Dr. Paul Yonggi Cho

Communing with the Holy Spirit

(How can anyone faithfully pray for hours and hours on end?)

I pray because I can have communion with the Holy Spirit only through prayer. When I ask people to pray, people say, "Pastor, we couldn't pray too long. We're supposed to pray for one hour, but when we look at our watches, it is only ten minutes! We don't have enough material to pray that long. How can you pray for one or two hours?"

The longer your pray, the more influence of the Holy Spirit will be present. Without praying one hour or more, you can't really say you are full of the Holy Spirit when you get up to speak. Please, forgive me, but that is my experience. If I don't pray for at least one hour, I can't say I can be prepared for a message. If you just sit down for one hour without mentioning anything — that is not prayer. Prayer is speaking to God, praising God and also hearing from His side.

"How can you keep praying for more than one hour?" people ask and I answer, "It's very easy! I have a spiritual jogging course. You can make a course of a half-hour, one hour, two hours. After you lay out the course you should go around it. To prepare a longer time, you must prepare yourself. For example, when I use my one-hour jogging course, I start by praising God, thanking Him for everything He did yesterday — detailing those things. After I praise Him for that, then I ask Him to bless today's programs. I sum up all of today's items and ask Him to bless my ministry today. Then I pray for my church. I pray for my half-million members because, even though I don't have that many now, I pray as if they are already there. For some time, I have been envisioning a million members, so to me that many is actual. People can't see, but I'm pregnant — my church is growing inside of me. It is so real that I can see a million Christians.

Then I pray for my cell leaders. After that I pray for all of my departments and my church. Then I come to America by prayer. I pray for Mr. Reagan, the senators and congressmen and the people in the American church and all my TV viewers. Next I go over to Japan and pray from Okaida to Okinawa and I ask God to take out the old idols and send the devil to Russia! I ask God to convert Japan and send them by the scores to China to lead the Chinese people to Jesus.

I pray for my TV program in Japan and my crusade all over the Japanese nation. That is my one-hour jogging course. When I conclude with Japan, I have finished exactly one hour.

When I have more time I go into my two-hour course and I pray specifically for my construction program. We are enlarging the church to seat 25,000 thousand people and we are going to finish it by next year so I am praying about the construction and the problems involved. I also pray for my broadcasts into Korea — I am broadcasting by radio and TV.

Then I pray for my father and mother. I have four brothers and four sisters so I pray for them. I pray for my wife and my three boys and for myself. That becomes my two-hour jogging course.

You must decide on your jogging course and use it so you

can pray 30 minutes, one hour or two hours very easily. The more time you spend before the Lord, the more of the Holy Spirit you will feel. You need the communion of the Holy Spirit! Many people know theologically that the Holy Spirit is with them, but practically they are not really knowing how to have that communion.

Jesus said, "Words shall not receive the Holy Spirit and recognize the Holy Spirit," but the Bible says, "You will recognize Him because He will be with you and He will be in you." That means you will recognize Him.

What does it mean to "recognize Him"? How could you say you recognize me? When you see me, you say, "Oh, you are Cho from Korea! How are you?"

That means that we should also recognize the Holy Spirit in our ministry and tell Him, "Holy Spirit, I welcome You." Praise God! Then the Bible says, "He shall be with you." You know, "with you," means you've got to welcome Him. If someone is with you, then you should welcome them!

The Bible also says, "He is in you." That means He is the source of your power and your wisdom and knowledge, so you should depend on Him. I always say to my people, "Recognize the Holy Spirit. Welcome Him and depend on Him because the Bible says you will recognize Him and He will be with you and in you."

In 1964 when I was pioneering my second church, I accumulated 3,000 members. I pushed and pulled and did everything, but my ministry was stalled. My vision-dream then was to have 10,000 members because at that time in Korea the Presbyterians had the largest Christian church with 6,000 members. I went to the Presbyterian church and took the measurements from the pulpit and from side to side. The janitor came to me and asked, "What are you doing?"

I said, "I'm measuring because I'm going to build a slightly bigger church."

He told me, "You're crazy!"

But I said, "I'm not crazy. I'm sincerely making this church my model — only a little bigger."

I planned a few more rows of chairs than the Presbyterian church. Then I began to pray really hard to expand, but after 3,000 members I couldn't seem to grow beyond that. I struggled and struggled, but nothing happened.

After an early morning prayer meeting in the cold winter, I was left alone in the corner of the church and I was really pouring out my heart.

Suddenly I fell into a deep slumber. Usually in the cold weather you don't go into a slumber because it is too cold and we have no central heating system in the church. But I fell into a deep sleep and in my sleep I was in the presence of God. He spoke to me very clearly in my spirit. He said, "My son, answer My question. Suppose the Israelites were sent out into the wilderness to catch quail. How many quails do you think they might have caught?"

I asked, "Wilderness? There aren't many quail in the wilderness, and if they'd have gone out without any instrument, I don't think they would have caught many quail and I think many of them would have died of sunstroke."

Then the Spirit said to my heart while I was still in a deep slumber, "When I sent My wind — how many quail did they catch?"

"Oh, the quail were falling like dust on the camp!"

Then the Spirit said, "Don't you think I can do the same thing for you? You are pushing and pulling and using all kind of psychological things to get the sinners saved, but you are almost destroying yourself in the process. Don't you think I can send the Holy Spirit and let the sinners fall like dust on your camp?"

But I said, "Oh, God, I have the Holy Spirit. I'm born again. I have the Holy Spirit in me. I've received the fullness of the

Holy Ghost so I have the experience, too. But, Holy Spirit, do I need more?"

Then the stern rebuke came to me, "That is your trouble! The Holy Spirit is more than an experience. The Holy Spirit is an awesome Person and you have never lifted His personality." That message was so sharp that I awoke out of my slumber. But it made a deep change in my life.

I thought, "Huh? Do I treat the Holy Spirit only as an experience?" When I realized I did, a whole new revelation came into my heart.

Chapter 8

Dr. Paul Yonggi Cho

Prayer changes difficult people

(Like you and me!)

When I got married, my whole desire was to become an evangelist and so, after less than one week of marriage, I left my bride to go out on the evangelistic field. I bought an apartment house and left her there in charge of the operation and I took off. I kept on doing that for six months. Every Saturday, I would come back and after Sunday, I would leave again.

My wife was very unhappy. In the Orient, women are trained to serve their husbands and they really believe they are in need of their husbands, and so, when I first got married, my wife treated me very nicely. She'd give me a massage when I came back and she would warm the bath water in the tub and she would give me a scrub and all the kinds of things that you don't find women doing for their husbands in the Western world!

But the trouble nowadays is that your TV has changed the thoughts of the younger women and the Korean women are no longer doing this. They are spoiled.

My wife was depressed and she wasn't doing anything. Then one day my mother-in-law called me and

I knew something was wrong. When your mother-in-law calls, you're in trouble. She asked, "Do you like living with my daughter?"

I said, "Yes, I am a pastor. I could never divorce her. Why?"

"You took her and you married her and left her alone in a home and you have no fellowship with her. She's grieved."

I said, "She should know better. She should understand. She married a preacher."

I went home and said, "Wife, come over here. You went to your mother and you told her a funny story, so I am going to help you." I laid my hand on her and said, "You devil, come out!"

I thought I could simply help her like this but the devil never did come out! She became worse and she was completely depressed, so I was alone. One day I was really praying and I said, "Oh, God, I should always make Your ministry my first priority. How can I handle this situation? My wife is grieved. She's depressed and I don't know how to handle this. I have very good priorities in the order of my life because I take You first, my church second, me third, my children fourth and my wife fifth."

God said, "You must change the order of your life."

I asked, "How?"

God said, "I must come first, you come second, your wife should come third, your children fourth and your ministry last."

I said, "Oh, this devil from America! American pastors can accept that kind of order, but since we are better ministers, we can't accept."

But God said, "No. You may build the largest church in the world, but again — if your children become unhappy and get lost in the world — where is your church? You should build the church in your home before you build outside of your home. Renew fellowship with your wife. Get close to your wife. If you lose your wife, you are going to lose your foundation."

I came to my wife and said, "Well, honey, every Monday will be your day to do whatever you like."

But I did not know what I was really saying. The next Monday, she took me to the park. She wanted me to become a romantic young man and walk around holding her hand and telling her romantic things. My mind was full of the ministry and the country. She was talking and talking, but I was not even listening. Then she took me to a department store. While we were window-shopping, I was dying. I said, "I'll give you all the money to buy."

But she said, "Don't you just enjoy looking at things?'

Then we went off to eat together and it was a real labor. So I had my first fellowship with her that day and, since I kept on having fellowship, she pulled out of the depths of depression. Through that I found out it is one thing to be legally married, but it is something else to have deep fellowship and really know each other.

The Holy Spirit brought that situation to re-membrance and reminded me, "You have a knowledge of the Holy Spirit, but you have never come into a deep fellowship with Him. You are alone — fighting in your flesh."

I said, "How can I have fellowship with the Holy Spirit?"

"Welcome the Holy Spirit because He is with you. If you have a guest in your home — don't you welcome him?"

"Yes, I welcome him."

"Then welcome the Holy Spirit. He's in you. Depend on Him."

That day I said, "Dear Holy Spirit, I was afraid to mention You. Of course, I was glad to sing about You — praising and praying to You in songs, but I was afraid to pray to You in conversation because I was never taught to pray to You in such a way in Bible school. I was instructed to pray to the

Father in the name of Jesus Christ; I was never taught to pray to You."

I thought, "Who is the Lord of the harvest?"

When I looked in Acts 13, it is clear that when Paul prayed, the Holy Spirit spoke, "Choose Paul and Barnabas for my ministry and my work for the Holy Spirit is the Lord of the harvest." Even Jesus said, "Pray to the Lord of the harvest so that the Lord of the harvest shall send more laborers into the field."

Also the "communion of the Holy Spirit" is talked about by the apostle in 1 John 1:3. "Our fellowship with the Father and His Son Jesus Christ." In the Greek language that fellowship is known as "Koinonia" and Paul asked the Corinthians to use the same communion with the Holy Spirit. Exactly as we have communion with the Father and the Son, we should have the communion of the Holy Spirit. The Father is on the throne; Jesus Christ is on the right hand and the Spirit of the Lord is with us together as evidenced in the love of God and the grace of Jesus Christ and He is active in the ministry. He is ready to impart vision, knowledge, wisdom and guidance in everything. He's here — so let's recognize Him!

Any person who visits my home and is not recognized, will be grieved. If a person lives with me and I don't really recognize him, he will be quenched. For this reason I foster fellowship with my wife. I recognize her. I welcome and appreciate her — purposely! After living with my wife for more than twenty years, I don't feel that early attraction I felt when we first married, but in the morning when I get up, I turn and say, "Dear, I love you." Before she gets up and makes up her face and hair, she is not so beautiful to see! I don't always feel like saying it, but I reach out my hand and say, "I love you." I tell her she is beautiful even though she is now pleasingly plump.

She says, "I am too fat," but I console her by saying, "There's more to love." By fostering our fellowship, I can love her more and the Spirit is with us.

As with my wife, I need to welcome Him and depend on Him.

From that day on I have said, "Dear Holy Spirit, good night. I really appreciate that You help me preach the Gospel of Jesus Christ."

Prayer Can Help You Have a Good Day

(Not to Mention a Good Life!)

In the morning I say, "Dear Holy Spirit, it is a wonderful day. You are my Senior Pastor, my Senior Administrator. With Your help, together we are going to preach Jesus today."

When I write my sermon, I say, "Dear Holy Spirit, let's go. Help me. Anyway, You've got to preach through me, so You'd better let me know about Your secrets!"

Then, when I go to the platform, I say, "Dear Holy Spirit, let's go! I depend upon You. You and I are going to preach this message together. I depend on You."

Then, when I finish my sermon, I say, "Dear Holy Spirit, I appreciate You. You did a wonderful job out of that mess. I thank You!"

I was purposely fostering the fellowship of the Holy Spirit because He is a Person I cannot see physically, but I was treating Him like a Person.

I asked Him, "Anoint me so that I can pray a powerful

prayer. Let's go to preach." I talked to Him in such a way that I began to feel His presence deeply in my life. I began to feel a new dimension of power and inspiration.

Suddenly my church of 3,000 people began to pick up. We went to 6,000, then 12,000 and in 1969 when we reached 18,000 members, God said: "Cho, resign from the church. Go to the island and build the largest church in the world."

In 1973 I built that church. I have been in it for over ten years. Once again we have built a church from scratch to more than more than a half-million active members. We screen out inactive members monthly through our cell systems and we would never leave dead cells. Many of the churches still have members who are buried in the cemetery, but their names are left on the rolls. We don't have that because we only consider members active if they are involved in the cell system. Our more than a half-million members are active and regularly attend services.

Through the communion of the Holy Spirit, my ministry began to suddenly take off and I began to have a powerful outreach. For this reason I am desperately depending on the Holy Spirit. Even today, when I speak in America, I say: "Dear Holy Spirit, let's go. You know that English is not my mother tongue and so I do not speak good English." I have to depend on the Holy Spirit to lead me even concerning my language. I've been living this way most of my life — always depending and leaning on the Holy Spirit. If anything happens in my ministry, I must give the praise to the Holy Spirit and Jesus Christ.

Through His help I have been enabled to lead this great church. Communion with the Holy Spirit leads me to victory.

To summarize: prayer is the channel through which God interferes in human affairs. If you don't pray, God will bypass you. Look at the blind Bartimaeus. He was begging on the street and Jesus Christ had already passed him by when Bartimaeus began to cry, "Oh, Son of David, be merciful unto me." People said, "Jesus has already gone by. It is no use for you to cry," but he kept on shrieking and shouting.

Jesus Christ stopped and turned around and came to help in the blind man's life. And so, when you pray, you are inviting Jesus Christ into your situation; into your affairs. From 1969 to 1973 I passed through the worst darkness of my life when God commanded me to build the largest church in the world. At that time I had $3,000. With faith I went and purchased the land by credit from the city and I also made a contract to build a church to seat 10,000 people without having any money to do so.

At that time I was also building a condominium so I needed around $2 million. To a small Korean that was a very big amount of money. To Americans it would not be so much. You are rich people. But to us, it is a great amount of money.

By faith I started. When they brought the bulldozers in and were tearing up the place like Lake Michigan, I was struck with fear. They were really there, doing the work to build a church for 10,000 people! Surely I must be joking!

As they started to dig the ground, the whole thing hit me with great impact. I thought, "How are you going to pay? Every month the bill is going to come and you will be responsible to pay for it!"

I was struck with reality.

When I closed my eyes, I could believe.

When I opened them, I could not.

I had bills to pay.

But I had no money.

What was I supposed to do?

I spent more time with my eyes closed than open. I was afraid to see the situation.

When they began bringing the material in to start the building, I knew I was absolutely dependent on the promises of Jesus Christ. I said, "God, You asked me to build and You are my chief resource."

To make matters worse, factories began to close down! Banks began to close. People began to lose their jobs. The offering just zoomed down. Mr. Nixon devalued the American money and the Korean economy was fluctuating after the American currency. When the American dollar catches cold, the Japanese money starts sneezing and the Korean currency catches pneumonia. Because of all this, we are so dependent on America in our economy. When Mr. Nixon devalued the American dollar, I began to lose hundreds of thousands of dollars and the contractor wanted to devalue their contracts. I was swimming in an ocean of fear and I knew I was drowning. There seemed absolutely no place for me to turn. Bills were piling up. I was not receiving enough income. I was at the end of my rope.

Some of the leaders of my congregation became Job's friends. They said, "We knew you were going to fail. You should have never started that kind of risky business. You are crazy! You are drowning!" When you are drowning, people are very glad to cry with you. When you are successful, they are very stingy with their praise. It is easier to cry together than to rejoice together over success. Many came to cry and comfort me, but I knew I was drowning.

The only resort that I could turn to was God. The building stood unfinished, the iron frame was rusting. I sat under the iron frame one day as the rain dripped from it and I said, "Lord God, why don't You let this iron beam drop and crush me and kill me so that I can have a justified reason not to pay the debt?"

To me, humanly speaking, there seemed no way of escape or survival. I wanted to die. "Oh, God," I wailed, "let me die!" I asked, "Where are You?"

Suddenly, though, my people became wiser than their pastor. They said, "Let's pray for our pastor. He's dying. Let's get together and pray." And so, they began to gather together to pray. They'd come directly from their businesses and go to the basement of the unfinished church without even going home. Right on the cement floor they knelt down and prayed. I said, "Foolish!" I began to lose my faith. "If this is the result of my faith, I must have heard a wrong voice."

As the people prayed, they begged: "Pastor, come over and pray."

I answered, "Most of you are poor people with no job, no money. Can God write a check? There's no way!

But they said, "You taught us to pray!" And so, I was pulled into their prayer. First a few hundred came, then a few thousand and one thing happened to change things. An 80-year-old grandmother, one who lived alone and had no children left and was living on the meager support of the government, came forward crying and trembling. She held up an old newspaper in front of my people. She said, "Pastor, you have been so good to us. You have been teaching me and I have been saved and I love you, but I can see you are dying in this church. What can we do but pray? We ought to do something — at least five bread and two fish and then expect a miracle. All I have in this world is this beat-up rice bowl and two chopsticks. If I had any money, I would give everything, but this is all I have in my life. I am eating out of this every day, but I can eat out of cardboard and I can eat with two fingers. All I have I give to the Lord. I can't just sit down and pray. I've got to do something."

How could I accept this from a grandmother? She was crying and I was crying. I thought, "I'll act like I received these things." And then I said, "You can't eat without a rice bowl and chopsticks. Please take these home."

She crumpled down crying and said, "Pastor, this is not a

worthwhile money tree, but my life is in this place. Wouldn't God accept this kind of gift from an old, dying widow? I love you! I want to see you delivered from this predicament!" She began to weep some more.

Then a businessman stood up and declared, "I'll give $10,000 for that rice bowl."

Another businessman declared, "I'll give $20,000." Another one said, "I'll give $30,000 for that rice bowl." Then the rice bowl began to fly! The Spirit of the Lord came down and people began to weep. One by one they began to stand up and they said, "I'll give my home. I'll go to the apartment house. I'll give the balance to the church."

Then a young couple stood up and said, "We'll give four years of our earnings. We'll live by faith." By that evening the $2 million was pledged. Out of nothing, out of the clear blue sky, it came.

Then God began to pour down His blessings. Soon the oil began to flow and the American dollar began to regain its power and people began to get jobs and our people began to prosper in their jobs and their businesses. They became so prosperous and so blessed.

In 1973 when Billy Graham came, he held a ministers' conference in my church. God is very humorous — 13,000 international ministers came and packed out the place and every one of them came and shook hands with me and said, "We knew that you could make it a success. We knew!"

If only they knew — it came only through prayer. Jesus had already passed by on the Jericho road. He'd already passed by me, but since my Christians stopped and prayed, He said: "Come over, Cho. I'll give you some blessings." Not by sending a millionaire, but by sending that old, dying widow with the beat-up rice bowl that shook up the whole place and the devil was broken and the people began giving of their own and God blessed the ministry and the lives of the people.

That was an unforgettable experience in my life. People say, "We are poor — we have nothing to give." That is a lie! If you do the best you can do, then what you cannot do, God will take charge of!

Only through prayer can this be enabled.

And so, I can tell you — spiritual growth starts on your knees. You can apply all kind of gimmickry and techniques and psychological pushing and pulling, but if you don't pray, they will all be as nothing. When you literally kneel down and pray and break the power of Satan, then God's Holy Spirit is going to move in on you and God is going to use the five loaves of bread and two fish to bless all the people.

Let's pray! Organize a structured prayer program and you will give a genuine impact to your neighborhood, to your town and to your city. The power of God is going to come and hover over you. Things are going to happen by the Holy Spirit because the Bible says, "Born of flesh is flesh, but only born of the Spirit is spirit." All of our evangelistic efforts under human flesh is our flesh, but when you pray, you are going to reactivate the promises of the Bible by the power of the Holy Spirit!

Chapter 10

Dr. Paul Yonggi Cho

Faith is your foundation

(... And it thrives in the uncertainty of the unknown!)

Some ministers have come up to me and asked, "How do you live day after day — getting up so early?"

The secret: I always try to take a nap after lunch! If you don't take a nap, your strength would be completely drained off and you wouldn't be living too long!

Faith is the foundation as far as everything in heaven is concerned. Faith always thrives in the elements of the unseen by our sense knowledge. Also, faith always prospers in utter uncertainty. If we ever want to know about the future, then we must try to use faith or we lose our qualifications. We are just launching out by faith in an unknown, unseen, uncertain world. That has been my experience about faith, so that is why I want to share about it.

Many people come to me. I hear, "You say to have faith, but I don't feel faith." But, brothers and sisters, faith was planted by the Holy Spirit in your heart when you received Jesus Christ as your personal Savior. The Bible says in Romans 12, verse 3: "God has given every man a measure of faith." So, whether you feel it or not, the Bible says you were dealt a measure of faith when you received Jesus Christ as your personal Savior and you were given the faith to believe God.

When you accept Jesus Christ, then you are given the ability and capacity to believe in the living God. That is a gift of faith imparted to your heart by the Holy Spirit. Usually people say, "Well then, we have such small faith. Will such a small faith ever work?"

Yes, small faith works. It is not a matter of whether you have a small or a great faith, but it is how you use it. Many people have faith dormant in their lives. One day one of my friends came to me and gave me a package of mustard seed. Mustard seed is so small, it is like a speck of dust. I was so pleased. I wanted to show the mustard seed to my congregation so I brought the seed to my early morning prayer meeting. That day about 600 people came out to the church. After preaching, I lined them up so they could see the mustard seed by passing in front of the platform. I was showing them that it looked like dust on the Bible. One by one they looked and they shook their heads. An old lady came and said, "Pastor, I can't see."

I told her, "Come closer."

"I still can't see," she said.

All the mustard seeds had been blown away by her breath! I was frantic — I tried to gather them back but once the tiny seeds were mixed with the dust, I couldn't find one of them!

I was aggravated until the Spirit spoke to my heart, "Son, don't get angry. If those mustard seeds were so small that they could be blown away by the breath of an old lady, then you should not worry about the size of your faith. If you have faith the size of one of these small seeds, you can cause a tremendous mountain to be removed to yonder sea."

And so, it does not matter about the size of your faith. It matters how to develop it in a practical life. Here I hope to show you the practical way to utilize the faith that you have. Throughout my 26 years of ministry, God has really taught me the principles of faith. Of course I have failed so many times. Through failure — through thick and thin — God taught me the practical side of faith and I am delighted to live in faith.

The Bible says, "Faith is the substance of things hoped for, the evidence of things not seen" (Hebrews 11:1).

To develop faith in your spiritual growth, you've got to give the "things" a clear-cut goal. Faith requires a clear-cut goal. It's the substance of things hoped for. If you don't have things, you don't give any substance to your faith. We can never pray without any substance. Faith is the substance of things. If you don't have clear things, then your faith is there, but your faith has no substance.

Faith is like your arm. If your arm has nothing to reach for and grab hold of, then your arm is hanging useless on you shoulder. When you have a clear-cut goal or objective, then your arm can rise up and reach out and grab hold of that objective.

Faith is like that. You are not going to feel faith every moment. I don't need to constantly feel my arm hanging on my shoulder. When I want to reach for something, then I need to feel my arm moving toward that goal. I don't always feel faith.

Nowadays I believe that God has given me a larger amount of faith. Today my belief that my church will reach a million members is like piecemeal. I can believe very easily with no strain to my heart.

I can even believe for 2 million easily because I've grown in faith. But I don't feel that faith in my heart. I have no exciting, burning sensation going through my backbone.

Many people say to me, "Oh, I want to feel the faith." So far I have never felt that kind of faith. I've always felt icy-cold in my heart. Still, I have always exercised faith and God has answered me in such a magnificent way.

To really practice faith, you must have that clear-cut goal. Faith is the substance of things.

In 1958, I graduated from Bible college and went out to the suburban area of Seoul to start a church. I had a tremendous desire to build a big church, but my capacity of faith was very small. I could only believe for 150 people. With all the faith that I could mobilize in my heart, I could only think of 150. So I prayed over and over, "Lord, if I can have 150 members in my church, I will never complain to You about my black hair turning white. I'll be satisfied eternally!"

That was my uttermost goal. At that time I didn't even dream that I could have a half-million members. No way! So I was vaguely asking God to give me around 100 or 150.

I worked very hard. I went from house to house and was preaching with a real fervency in my spirit, but no one came to listen to me. (That was my trouble!) In less than five months all my ministerial material had dried up. I'd used all my sermon topics. Then I became frantic. I borrowed old messages from Billy Graham ... those dried up also. I spoke all of Oral Roberts' messages and those dried up also. After preaching six months, I was quite sure I was not called into the ministry, because I had nothing to preach!

I tried to create sermons from Genesis to Revelation, but I couldn't make one sermon. I began to believe I had not been called into the ministry. In less than one year I had packed up eight times to leave my ministry. I was preaching to the empty tent cathedral week after week, and I was depressed.

One day I was reading Scripture and became greatly encouraged by reading in Mark 11:23(RSV). "Truly, truly I say unto you, That whosoever shall say unto this mountain, Be thou removed, and be thou cast into the sea; and shall not doubt in his heart, but shall believe that those things which he saith shall come to pass; he shall have whatsoever he saith."

I thought "Oh, If I can command a mountain to be removed, then I think I can apply this faith in my practical life." At that time I was going day after day without eating food because I had no support. (After the Korean War, I was absolutely poverty stricken.) I knelt down and said, "Lord, God, please supply my daily need. I need a table, a chair, and a bicycle to ride on. I need at least those things, and You are rich, God. According to my faith I am not going to remove mountains, but I want to bring a table, chair and bicycle into my life." And I believed.

I was waiting. I waited one month. Nothing happened. I thought, surely next month God will deliver. Nothing happened. I waited a third month, fourth month, fifth month. Still nothing happened. Finally, I was tired of waiting.

One evening, totally discouraged and crying, I prayed, "Lord, it is one thing to know the Word of God. It is entirely another thing to practice it. If I can't receive an answer to prayer, how can I ask these poverty-stricken people to believe in You? I would be a hypocrite if I asked them to believe in Thee for their practical life."

Then some tremendous sensation — tranquility — came over me. Oh, the peace and joy! Outside I was crying, but inside I was rejoicing because of the Presence of peace. Then a revelation came. Not in an audible voice I just knew. And understanding was given and I felt enlightened. The Spirit seemed to say to my heart, "My son, I've heard your prayer and I've answered."

But where were my chair, table and bicycle? Then the understanding came to me, I've answered you tentatively, but still I am waiting for you to be more specific. Don't you know there are dozens of kinds of tables, dozens of kinds of chairs, dozens of kinds of bicycles? You have asked for a table, chair and bicycle — what kind? I am waiting until you become specific, until then ... I can't answer you.

I said, "Prove that by the Bible. Is this a revelation from the Lord? Show me in the Bible."

Then the revelation came to me. In Hebrews 11, I read verse one. Up until that time I'd never seen that in Hebrews. The Spirit made me rivet on the word "things."

Faith is the substance of things.

I couldn't read any longer. The Spirit said, "Look at the word things. If you have definite things, you are going to have definite faith. You have very vague things right now, so God cannot supply. Suppose you go to a department store and ask the owner, 'Please give me something.' Would you receive anything? If you insisted, they would send you to the insane asylum. If you should be specific when you want to buy something from a department store, then even more, you should be very specific when practicing your faith in My presence."

That was a life-changing experience! I said, "Father, no one taught me in the Bible to pray along that line, but now I am understanding. I am sorry that I misunderstood You. I officially cancel all my past prayers. I would like to start all over."

I knelt down and prayed, "God, I want to have a table (and I told Him the size) made of Philippine mahogany, and I want to have a chair with an iron frame that rolls around so I can push it around like a big shot. Then I want to have a bicycle made in the U.S.A. Father, now I've made all these things so clear that You can't make any mistakes on those articles, and I'm waiting."

I was excited because those things were so clear to me then! Up until that time I was so vague. But since I made my order so clear to the Lord that I could see them in my imagination, I was sure that God was going to give me those things. I was praising God and, sure enough, in a few months, one by one, those things came into my possession — the table of Philippine mahogany ... the chair with the iron frame and rolling tip ... then the bicycle made in the U.S.A. (and slightly used by a missionary child) were all supplied to me.

Such a life-changing experience. I thought, this is really working! I've had faith all through these days, but I did not know how to exercise my faith. Now I know. At that time I began to apply that principle of faith in my ministry.

I said, "Lord, up to this time I've been praying bless my church, bless my ministry, bless my family." What kind of blessing out of 7,000 promises in the Bible?

I wrote down numbers and said, "Oh, God, before the end of this year I want 150 members in my church. I know, You know, so I believe." Since faith is the substance of things hoped for, and I gave God the things, my faith had substance to work with and I could really believe. I could feel the tension of faith in my heart. I believed and I claimed and I worked and, behold, at the end of that year I had 150 saved.

When I had 150, I said, "Who wants to spend the rest of his life with 150? Oh, God, I did not know that I was having the faith. Now I want to believe for a greater number."

Because of my experience my faith had grown! (Through experience the sinew of your faith becomes stronger.) Then it was easier to believe for 300. I asked God for 150 more in the next year — beyond 300 I could not believe. At that time I thought 300 would be my limit, so I said, "Oh, God, when I have 300 that will be the plateau for my church growth. I will be so happy!"

My faith rose up and began to work powerfully. By the end of the year I had the 300, and I asked again, "Who could be satisfied with 300?" As my faith began to become experienced, my faith began to grow. I could believe for 600!

Beyond that, with faith and the Holy Spirit, it was easy for me to believe for 3,000 members. So I stood up in church and declared, "Now, I believe for 3,000 members!" My people laughed, for they thought I was becoming proud and arrogant after having 300. People said, "Now he's imagining too much!" Even my girlfriend came to me and said, "If you keep on saying you will have 3,000, I will leave you."

But I replied, "You don't understand me."

"Of course I don't understand you. How could you have 3,000 under this tent church? The largest church in Korea has 6,000, so how can you — green bean out of Bible college — have 3,000 in such a quick way?"

"Grace, believe in me. I have the faith."

She cried, "People are calling you 'old kook'!"

"Whether people call me a kook or not, I believe. I have the capacity to have it happen."

No one can estimate the faith you have. Only the Spirit knows your limit. I believed for 3,000! That was in 1960, and by 1964, I had the 3,000.

There should be no limit in church growth. There should be no plateau until the last soul is saved in your area. In church ministry you've got to use your faith.

The Bible says it shall be done unto you according to your faith. It is impossible to please God without having faith. He can only intervene into your realm through the channel of faith.

Of course, education and organization are very good, but education and organization without faith would be dead things. When you hear the clear-cut goal, then faith is going to rise up and work.

Several years ago I was invited to go to Australia and speak to the General Council of the Australian Assemblies of God. When I went there, I learned that the standard of their faith was very low. In each Australian church, there were 20 to 30 members. One by one they came to me and said that there would be no church growth in Australia. Australia was too rich and too involved in sports and gambling, so the church would not grow. I knew the Australian church could grow, so during the conference I spoke about faith. Whether they were going to listen to me or not, I told what was on my heart. I shared the faith possibility.

They told me that in the Australian Assemblies of God the membership had grown less than two persons per pastor in ten years. The growth of two people was only biological growth. It was not really winning souls to Jesus Christ. They would have that many by giving birth to their own children! I told them about the principle of faith and the principle of church growth, but people were nonchalant toward my teachings and just sat there watching me. I could read their eyes.

Finally, before I left, I challenged them. "You may forget all my teaching in a week, but don't forget one thing. Please bring a sheet of paper and a pencil. I'm going to do a drastic work for you."

They brought the paper and pencil, and I said, "Now, I want you to write down your definite growth goals for five years. To have church growth you need to stay at one church at least five years. If you move every third year, you should forget about church growth. For this reason, you should write down your five-year goals. Ask the Holy Spirit to reveal to you and then see your faith ability rise up and grab hold. Paste the written goal on the wall and look at the goal every morning and every evening and declare you are going to have that goal. Do that — even if you don't like to listen to me. Give the goal of your faith and try it and see your faith rise up to conquer that goal." They all laughed. They said it was superstition.

I told them, "No, faith is the substance of things hoped

for, and if you don't have things to hope for, then your faith is going to have a long sleep in your heart. But if you claim a goal, then faith is going to have substance to work for and faith is going to be busy. Whether you believe it or not — try it! Write down the goal and read it and believe on it every day. The more you read, the better you are — so read!" I pronounced the benediction and left. In two years the Australian Assemblies of God Church had 50 percent growth. In two years! Now they are having a revival like a wild fire.

After the two years I was invited back once again. Three thousand interdenominational ministers and church leaders got together for a church growth conference. Later I brought whole planeloads of the leading ministers by Boeing 747 jet to Seoul, and I conducted a seminar for church growth through the cell system and Prayer Mountain. Then our Church Growth Institute members and I had a great church growth conference in Sydney, Australia. Now, wherever you go, you see Australian churches really on fire and mushrooming. The first time I was there, the largest church had between 100 and 200 members. Now there are several with 3,000 to 5,000!

In ministry, if you don't use your faith, then you can't have a miracle. Without your own faith you can't expect any miracle to happen. In my own personal ministry I have always exercised my faith for church growth. There are problems in Japan and I am determined to conquer Japan for Jesus. I think my responsibility for the rest of my life is to lead ten million Japanese souls to Jesus Christ. I am deeply determined, but still I am struggling. Over and over again I have conducted seminars for Japanese ministers, but they always give excuses. "Church growth is possible in America and Korea, but Japan is a different place."

I say, "Write down your faith goals," but they protest, "No, we are afraid. If we do not accomplish the goals you will be ashamed." If I could only persuade them to write down their goals, then something would happen. But they will not. They say, "We know that goal can't be accomplished."

Still I am struggling. I believe there will be victory sooner or later. The younger generation is studying and more or less obeying me.

When you have a clear-cut goal in you faith, then you have a clear sense of direction. Many churches have no sense of direction so they are wasting time, energy and money. When you have a clear-cut goal, you can converge all your time, energy and money into that focus.

Not only that, but when you have a clear-cut faith goal, then you can be motivated. When you know the mountain top, you are motivated to climb it. So that is our goal. Over and over I say to my congregation, "Our goal is there. Let's climb up." This year our goal is 200,000 new members to be added within the year. I speak over and over, "Two hundred thousand. That's our goal," to the Christians so that they can join their faith to my faith to believe for that goal.

I told you that we have more than a half-million members, but that is not exactly true. Every hour we are receiving around 500 new converts. Every hour! When I announce my statistic, it is already too late! We should correct them every hour because we have more than 20,000 cell leaders and they are winning souls every hour. The cells are winning converts in the apartment houses, marketplace and everywhere.

People come and look at my church and they say, "Wow! Big church! It is magnificent!" But I say, "You have a misunderstanding. This is not my church. My church is in an apartment house, in the village market-place, the college, the high school — my church is there! This building is just a celebration hall. Every Sunday we get together to celebrate the resurrection of Jesus Christ there, but this is not a church. Communists could come down and destroy this place at any moment. They may destroy the building, but they cannot destroy the church. The church is not in that building. The church is in the people.

Our church is growing around the clock — not just on Sunday. People are having a person-to-person touch. They are touching their neighbors and winning souls to Jesus Christ.

To put your faith to work, you must write down your faith goals. I challenge you to write down your personal and church growth goals. You've got to write them so your faith will rise up to work.

You must constantly supply nutrition to your faith. Your faith is a living thing, not a dead thing, and you should oil your faith and supply it with nutrition. How can you do this? By using the fourth dimension of sight-seeing. Instead of visions and dreams, I always use the word "sight-seeing." Visions and dreams are so philosophical — words that common people can't grab hold of. So I say the fourth dimension is sight-seeing. How can it be so?

Romans 4:17 says, "God, who quickeneth the dead, and calleth those things which be not as though they were." That is the nature of God. He transcends both time and space. God holds to things which are not, as if they are already here! If you ever want to work together with God, you should transcend your time and space. How could God bring future things into your present situation and speak as though they are already here? To do that, you must also learn how to go from the third dimension to the fourth dimension of visions and dreams. We are all dominated by the third dimension — we are dominated by time and space — past, present and future. But when you reach the fourth dimension, you go beyond the limitations of time and space. You are then going to be in the realm of the Holy Spirit.

As human beings, we are limited physically by the third dimension, but still we have a spiritual quality through which we can project ourselves into the fourth dimension so we can work together with God. Before you go into visions and dreams, you can't really work together with the Holy Spirit. The Holy Spirit belongs to the fourth or eternal dimension. The Holy Spirit is always present now, so the Holy Spirit wants to call those things which are not as if they were. You may predict your church growth as 3,000 members in five years, but the Holy Spirit calls the 3,000 as if you already have them now.

So there is trouble. You say, "I am going to have 3,000 in five years." The Spirit says, "No, you already have 3,000." To agree with the Holy Spirit, you are forced to go into your visions and dreams.

In order to cross over space and time limitations, I began to invent a new vocabulary. I always say that I am already pregnant with the 3,000 members — like a woman who is pregnant with a child.

During early pregnancy, you can't see it with your physical eyes, but you can feel it. I say, "I'm pregnant with 3,000. It shall take five years to give birth to 3,000, but I already have them growing inside me." If you don't have that kind of mental situation, you can't work together with the Holy Spirit.

I call it fourth dimension sightseeing. I sit down and calmly do sight-seeing. When you take the sight-seeing bus, you just sit down and relax and go around taking in the sights, don't you? Spiritually I do sight-seeing every day.

Right now we are in the middle of enlarging our church. I need a tremendous amount of money. We already have spent more than $10 million and I need $10 million more to complete. I shall receive the $10 million through the miraculous intervention of God. I must believe for that other $10 million and I must feed that faith constantly so that doubt will never come.

How do I do that? Even today I practice it from my Washington, D.C. hotel. I sit down, relax, praise God. Then

I go spiritual sight-seeing. I just take a fourth dimensional train and I go around and see my church completed. I see every part completely constructed, and I see the beauty of the church. I see tens of thousands of people flocking into the church. I rejoice and call those things which be not as if they were, together with the Holy Spirit. I say, "Dear Holy Spirit, it is it is finished. Money is bound to follow. The case is closed — so You are abound to supply the money. Praise God!" My faith becomes strengthened.

You don't need to continue grinding your teeth in perspiration and desperation. Relax. Take the bus of the fourth dimension and have spiritual sight-seeing — see the completed end result! You have the goal, but see it completed in your spirit. Get excited and saturated! Say, "Dear Holy Spirit, this is it! It is completed! Praise God!" That is how to strengthen your faith.

When Abraham was quite old, he was despondent because he couldn't have a child to bequeath his things to. God said He was going to give him a child, but Abraham was a great doubter. He said, "Oh, God speaks to me about a child in my old age? It's all baloney." He didn't believe, but God had a way to solve that predicament.

I read in Genesis 15:5-6 that God has a way of solving the problem. One night, Abraham was fast asleep in his tent and God woke him up. "Abraham, come out! Come out!" Abraham came out. "Look to the sky. Count the numbers of stars."

He began to count the stars and finally was swimming in the stars and the stars were swimming in him. He said, "Father, I can't count any longer." God said, "Your offspring are going to be as numerous as those stars."

Abraham was having spiritual sight-seeing. Suddenly all the faces of the stars seemed to be changing into the faces of children and he felt as if he were hearing the chorus, "Father Abraham!" He was profoundly shaken in his soul. He'd received a definite revelation of spiritual sight-seeing. After that he went back to his tent and tried to sleep. He buried his face into the pillow, but he could only see the faces of children — stars and stars and stars.

He was enjoying it so much, he was completely saturated in such warmth that he forgot he was almost 100 years old. He could see so many stars and so many children and his visions and dreams changed him so much that he began to walk like a young man! He began to talk like a young man. He was completely rejuvenated by visions and dreams, and he and his wife were able to produce Isaac.

Look at the Bible. It says, "And He brought him forth abroad, and said, Look now toward heaven, and tell the stars, if thou be able to number them: and he said unto him, 'So shall thy seed be." And verse six says, "He believed in the Lord; and he counted it to him for righteousness."

Abraham was a great doubter, but seeing the vision enabled him to believe. Faith came after the vision. Vision is the mother which is giving birth to faith. Do you see? If you can't believe — don't worry. Sit down, relax and have a spiritual sight-seeing. Once you suddenly are saturated with visions and dreams. Then you find you have been given the power to believe. Visions and dreams are the mother of faith.

In my own life, when a very difficult project comes and I am struggling to believe, I just go to Prayer Mountain and I crawl into the prayer grotto and relax myself. I have a spiritual sight-seeing; I see the project accomplished. I enjoy it because I don't feel any burden. It is really touring — in touring you don't get yourself all tensed up. So I sit down, relax and see stars and stars and stars and I say, "Oh, God, I see it completed. Completed! Praise God! It is completed!" And soon, because of this, I am given the power to believe.

Abraham saw the stars, then he believed. Before he saw the stars, he was a great unbeliever, but after seeing the stars, he became a believer, because visions and dreams give birth to faith.

You think you are making the visions and dreams, but I tell you, the visions and dreams are going to make you. That is the reason the Bible says, "Where there is no vision, the people perish." If you envision a church of 150, that vision will make you a pastor of 150. You will talk like the pastor of 150, sleep and walk like such a pastor. The vision is going to make your personality.

When I had 100,000 members, I began to believe for a half-million. I was experiencing spiritual sightseeing and I was excited. That vision transformed my personality completely. I was still pastor of a church of 100,000, but suddenly my personality changed as though I were the pastor of a half-million. I began to talk and walk and act like a pastor of a half-million. You can't help it! You are not making the vision; the vision is going to make you!

For this reason, I always say to the American people, "America, have a great vision for your nation." You are destined either to become a great nation or to turn into nothingness. I say, "America, please have a great vision for the whole universe." Then America will be given the power and the personality to lead the world.

I really worried about America after the Vietnam conflict, because the American people lost their vision. They became small people. Oh, the riots in the streets and the fighting in the schools! That made America look as though they were becoming a small rat instead of a big lion!

I'm glad the American people began to regain their visions and dreams. Great America! That vision is transforming personalities. Now when I look at the American society, the silent majority now has a lot of faith, confidence, the presence of the future.

You see, vision changes.

Even in your kids.

Faith can turn your children around
(Without your having to beat them!)

When your children are disobedient, don't just punish them! Pour in the vision day in and day out and they will be transformed. Vision is going to make them.

This year my son took an examination for the best university of Korea. Only a genius could enter that university! But my son was not a genius, he was nearer to being a fool — because he wouldn't study in high school. I begged him to study, but he was rebellious.

When I received his examination record (100 was a good mark), he received 30 to 40. My wife was frantic. She was arguing with him and beating him and he was fighting with her.

One day I was praying for my son, pouring out my heart. "Oh, God, what can I do?" God answered, "Don't rebuke him. Don't deal with him harshly just pour into his heart visions and dreams of what he can become.

After that, when he brought home his marks of 30 of 40, I

said to him, "Thirty? Much better than zero! Oh, you did a marvelous job!" Instead of being negative, I became positive. "It's marvelous! I believe if you will just add a little more effort — then you can make 50! If you can do better than zero, then you can make 50 next time."

He beamed. "Can I do that?"

"Yes, I believe it." I began to pour my visions and dreams into him day in and day out like God showed the vision to Abraham, the great doubter. And God knew how to deal with Abraham. He did not say, "Why can't you believe, you doubter? I'm going to kill you if you don't believe!"

But gently God called Abraham out and told him he was going to have a child. Abraham laughed and his wife laughed, but God knew how to correct him:

He called him out in the midst of the night and said, "Look at the stars. Don't look at your old age and dilapidated bodies. Count — keep counting. You are going to be the father of numerous children." God poured that vision into Abraham and that vision changed his personality. He believed God. Through that faith, God could come down and rejuvenate him. If you believe God, then through that faith God can do anything for you.

So, by using that method, I changed my son from a fool to a genius. Finally he began to study, make a fantastic record and entered the best university.

See? You can change things!

Even when I deal with my cell leaders, I do not rebuke them. I never say, "You're going to hell if you do that," nor do I tell them, "You're supposed to be a cell leader — what are you doing?" I never do that. I know the mistakes, but I try to find some good point of what they have accomplished and lift it up as a star.

"Look at this star — you did this and you can do better. You are a better person than you think. Look at the star! You can do it!" Then the people who have a low self-image and depression forget about their failures and look at the stars. Then their visions and dreams change.

You are not to make a vision. The vision is going to make you. For that reason, I try to get myself changed and by my own determination and fourth dimension sight-seeing, I can easily change myself. When I am so tired and don't feel like going out to preach, then I praise God and sit down and go fourth dimension sight-seeing. I see myself going to the platform; I see such excited people; I see myself preaching under the mighty anointing of God. I see so many souls saved and great things occur and I say, "Praise God! Wonderful ... wonderful ... wonderful!" So I find that I have been given the faith to rise up and preach.

God used this method over and over again. Seeing is very important; always seeing comes before possession. Look at Lot — Lot lifted up his head and looked to the vale of Jordan — Sodom and Gomorrah. That vision transformed his personality and put a desire in his heart and he went down to Sodom and Gomorrah. The vision did it.

At the same time, the Bible says, Lot's Uncle Abraham was in Palestine. He lifted up his head and looked to the north and south and east and west, and he had a vision. "Oh, I'm going to have this land!" This vision transformed him and now his children have Palestine.

Look at Lot's wife. He sternly warned, "Don't look at Sodom and Gomorrah." By looking back, one can create negative visions and dreams, and that can overpower the personality. When they were rushing out of Sodom and Gomorrah, Lot and his two daughters never turned back to look, but his wife turned back and saw Sodom and Gomorrah burning. In her imagination, she began to see all the joys and physical happenings, and the sensual life there, and she was full of such visions. She was seeing the stars and the power of Sodom and Gomorrah came upon her and took over and she could not leave.

She was riveted there on the ground until she turned into a pillar of salt.

Seeing changes! The devil never deceived Eve in one word, you know. When you look at Genesis, you realize there were plenty of places for them to go, but Eve kept coming to the Tree of Knowledge of Good and Evil and staring at that fruit day in and day out. Adam had a responsibility: he could have controlled his wife. But he had no control and she kept looking at the fruit.

She was seeing and imagining. Then the devil came. "Oh, take part! You are going to become very wise." When her imagination, visions and dreams overtook her, she was transformed to rebel against God. She reached out and took the fruit to eat.

If you would like to have church or personal growth, you should have that goal clear and make a star. Look at the star day in and day out. Don't look at yourself and say, "I lack education" or "I'm not an eloquent preacher." Don't say that.

As a preacher in Korea, I am one of the worst kind because I speak with a very strong southern accent. Since I minister in the Seoul area, people are always telling me, "We should come to your church three times consecutively to understand you."

Many times that has depressed me and I have tried to learn the Seoul vocabulary from my wife, but since I learned the southern accent by the milk of my mother, I can't change. I still speak a strong southern accent, people in North Korea and the northern area cannot understand me too well. Still, the people are coming.

If you would like to see a Christian in Seoul, it is very easy. Whenever you see Christians running with a Bible on Sunday, they are coming to my church! Because, if they don't run, they can't even have a standing space. They wait in line for one hour even in the frigid cold winter to have a place to stand.

Why should they come? Not only do I preach to meet their need, but I exercise my faith — and I see the stars! I'd been seeing our half-million people for five years. Every day I took the fourth dimension bus and did the sight-seeing. I saw a half-million. Half a million! Beautiful! Beautiful! Oh, God, beautiful! Then suddenly, I found I had a powerful faith in my heart for a half-million. Then when I stood in the pulpit, the faith for a half-million flowed out of me like a mighty river — so powerful that I knew that we were going to become a 500,000-member church. And we did!

Faith is contagious, so all of our Christians began to profess that faith. So having more than 500,000 is nothing. To me, a half-million is nothing. I can now predict for a million members, but I have no place to put them!

You grow faith, get nutrition by practicing fourth dimension sightseeing.

Your faith needs to be declared. Many people have faith by the fourth dimension sight-seeing and they get excited, but their faith is not working because they don't release their faith. How do you release your faith? By speaking with your mouth! If you don't declare boldly, then your faith is not going to be there, your faith is not going to be released as a creative power. Look at Jesus Christ. He always healed people by the spoken word. Look at the life of the apostles. When they healed the sick, they didn't pray, but they healed by the spoken word. Word went out and healed.

In Romans 10:10, the Bible says, "For with the heart man believeth unto righteousness; and with the mouth confession is made unto salvation." By declaring, saving faith will become realized. When you have faith, you release your faith by mouth confession and that mouth confession makes your position that of standing on a no-return bridge. In Korea, there is a no-return bridge. When you cross over, you are going to North Korea and you will never return. You're arrested. So by declaring, you pass through the no-return bridge.

When I first announced my plan that I was going to have a half-million members five years ago, all the elders and deacons trembled. But most of all, my wife trembled. She came back home and couldn't sleep. "What are you going to do? What are we going to become if you don't get a half-million? Why did you announce that? You could have kept it a secret in your heart. Why have you announced it?"

"If you don't put yourself in a predicament, God doesn't care too much about it."

In Korea, there was a famous Presbyterian minister who had a mighty healing ministry. He was completely convinced about the power of healing by reading the Scriptures. So one day he went out to practice. He went to the marketplace and found a crippled man. The preacher took him into a small alley. He looked around and, when he was certain no one was looking at them, quietly prayed, "In the name of Jesus — rise up and walk!" The crippled man did not stand. Instead, he angrily picked up a rock and cast it at the pastor. He never rose up because the pastor wanted to practice his faith in secret.

When you practice your faith in secret, you have nothing to lose. If you have victory or if you lose — that's fine. If you really want to exercise mighty faith, you must put yourself in a predicament in public. When you fail — everybody should know that you failed.

In public you have to mean business. You don't just jovially talk about it. You put everything into the project.

So when you release your faith, you should speak publicly!

Let God hear, let the devil hear, let Christians hear and even let unbelievers hear!

Five years ago, I declared my goal before God, before the devil, before Christians and before an unbelieving world. The newspapers wrote and jeered about me ... the Christians jeered at me ... and the devil scared me to death! Nobody believed in me, but I declared — trembling in my heart, my knees buckling — I was going to have a half-million people. I was so scared! Whenever I have launched a faith, I am the one who is scared the most.

But despite that fear, I launch it and God is merciful, because at least I have a thin faith.

God wants to see your faith publicly. Then you have great results. So I declared over and over again. I became so serious that I was training cell leaders and I was mobilizing finances and I was doing my best to accomplish it, because I was in a predicament. And God worked with me. Together now we are beyond the half-million mark!

Faith only works through bold-mouth confession. Release your faith boldly, declare it publicly and put yourself in a great predicament. Then you are going to be accepted by God as a believer.

Faith requires bold action. When you have a clear-cut goal and you have nurtured your faith by fourth dimension sight-seeing; then when you have boldly declared and released your faith and you have crossed over the no-return bridge — then you must act on your faith. You've got to do something. In acting your faith, timing is very important. You should not run ahead of God or pull back too far from God.

Look at the Apostle Paul who had the fervent desire to preach the Gospel to Asia, but failed in Asia. He wanted to go to Bithynia. Finally he came down to Troas and God showed him the vision of Macedonia. So, instead of going to Asia he went to Europe.

Wasn't it the will of God to preach the Gospel to Asia? Yes, but Paul wanted to go to Asia 2,000 years too early. God sent the Gospel to Asia through an American missionary to the specific area. Paul wanted to run 2,000 years ahead of God!

Was it the will of God? Yes. But timing is always very important. When Jesus Christ was at the wedding in Cana, his mother, Mary, said, "They do not have wine." Jesus told her, "It is not my time." He had all the power to change the water into wine, but He felt it was not His time. Timing is very important, and I have experienced many failures because I didn't keep the timing. I had all the faith, but I came ahead of God by ten or 20 years and I flatly failed. Now I know the timing. When you have a goal and the fourth dimension sight-seeing, and when you have declared — but when you pray you have this red light in your heart, the red light means restlessness. When you have restlessness, timing is not right. You should wait.

When you have a green light and have abundant peace — not heart peace — belly peace — when peace begins to swell up from your belly, then you know the timing has come. Regardless of your situation, you rise up and go.

Just before I came here, God gave me an idea. For a year now, God has given me the vision of a big rehabilitation center for young people. Even in Korea young people are becoming alcoholics and drug addicts. There are 10,000 young boys and girls roaming the streets in Seoul. God gave me the idea to help them, train them, get them jobs and make them good Christians. I was fumbling with the idea for one year in the fourth dimension sight-seeing and my faith became explosive! Then I declared, "I am going to build a home that can serve 1,000 young people and I want to feed them, train them and send them out." But our people were very worried because we need $10 million right now for completion of our church. To complete this youth home we need another $15 million. They would come to me and ask, "Where can you get the money?"

I am very, very dumb. For this reason, I don't carry a calculator. I don't worry about money. I worry about my faith. I am living by faith — and by faith God somehow always makes it happen. When Jesus asked Philip to feed the 5,000 men, he used his calculator. He said, "It's impossible. This is wilderness. We need more than 200 denarii in money ... We have no bakery ... Too late ... Impossible." Logical-minded. But Andrew, lacking a high IQ, just went out and got the five loaves and two fish. He said, "How this five loaves and two fish can feed 5,000, I don't know, but I brought them to You." He lacked IQ, but he had faith. If he hadn't the faith, he wouldn't have gone out and gathered the five loaves and two fish — such a foolish thing.

Philip might have said, "Andrew, I knew you were lacking on IQ, that's the reason why I didn't even call you as a member of the committee to study how to feed the 5,000 people, but I never dreamed you were lacking so much as to try to feed this many people with five loaves and two fishes!"

But Jesus Christ sided with Andrew and fed the people in the wilderness. People say, "This is the wilderness! The financial situation is very bad. This is no time to build a larger church. No!"

If you are a graduate student of the Philip's Seminary, you are down and out. If you are a graduate of the Andrew's School, you can still do! Scientists say a bumblebee should never be able to fly, but a bumblebee does not know — so he just flies! So many times I don't know where I can get money. My computer says I'm totally wrong. But — when I have faith — I just fly. That's all.

So, just before I came I was praying and God gave me the peace — the green light and I started building the youth center.

When I talked to my elders, they all dropped their heads and said, "Pastor, do we need $10 million for completion of our church? And another $15 million? Where can we get such money?"

"I don't know. My source is Jesus Christ. I have a green light. I have the goal I have nurtured through fourth dimension sight-seeing and my faith has become explosive. I announced and have crossed over the no-return bridge. Now I have peace, and I'm going. Let's go!"

I began to act. I went to the government; I went to the city; I went to find a location. Then I met the leading man in government. The Spirit said to me, "Ask him to donate the land — about 30 acres. Tell him you are not going to pay. Ask!"

So when I had lunch with this high-ranking government official who was in charge of this kind of thing, he already knew I was going to build a great youth house. I said, "I'm going to build a youth house and I need land. You've got to give me land." (In Seoul, it's very hard to get land.) "Right on the outskirts of Seoul — I should have a good location."

"Yes, we will try our best to find the location."

They found 30 acres on the outskirts of Seoul. The price was astronomical!

Then I said, "I need this land as a free gift in the name of Jesus Christ."

He looked at me intently and asked, "Are you crazy?"

"Yes, I am crazy. Otherwise I wouldn't have asked you in this way."

"Are you serious?"

"Yes, I'm serious. I already have permission from the highest authority."

"Who?"

"My Almighty God!"

Are you serious?" he asked again. "Are you all right?"

"Yes, I'm all right. I'm perfectly healthy."

"I'll go and discuss it with the highest authorities, also."

Before I left Korea, they sent word. "You can have the 30 acres — free of charge!"

It was worth millions and millions of dollars! Then the elders all came out to the airport, excited. They said, "Now we can see the vision! It is possible!" All things are possible to those who believe.

You can have a big church. Church growth doesn't just mean a big church, but to have a good quality you should have a good quantity.

You say, "I specialize in quantity." But I say, "I am a fisher of men." As a fisher I should catch a lot of fish to get good, good quality. Im not going around saying I just want to catch certain fish. I cast my net and get every kind of fish. Gathered together, I am not sure which is good quality. When you have a bigger crowd, you can have better quality. I believe in big things because the Holy Spirit believes in big things. At the day of Pentecost the Holy Spirit started with 3,000 members. Out of 200,000 people in Jerusalem at that time, the Holy Spirit made 3,000 converts. In one day — a 300,000-membership church. The next day, 5,000. The day after, a big crowd. I think, at the least, they had a church which had about 100,000 members in Jerusalem.

The Holy Spirit rejoices about the big number. If numbers mean nothing to God, why should the Bible mention about 3,000 and 5,000 people? He's concerned about numbers. We can have big numbers. This is my vision-dream.

Sooner or later across America, Christians will gather and you will see churches with 100,000 or 200,000 members before Christ returns. I believe it! If God can do that miracle in Korea, a traditional Buddhist country, He can do the same thing here. You are the ones that God wants to use!

Fellowship and blessings go hand-in-hand

(That's why you can't just worship at home!)

In Seoul the reason why we have such a growing church is because of the fellowship and evangelism through the cell system. In 1964 I had a very drastic experience in my life. I had 3,000 members and I had no associates other than my mother-in-law. She was my associate, but she was also a thorn in my flesh. Think of me working with my mother-in-law. It is a scary thing! I don't recommend you do that. She was a wonderful prayer woman, but she was very dominating — telling me to preach this way or that way. Still, I love her very much.

And so, I was exhausted. I was extending myself too much. I was a preacher, I was getting up early every morning to conduct the prayer meeting. I was doing home visitation. I was janitor, administrator. I began to think I couldn't stand it any longer. One evening, in the course of preaching, I became delirious and fell to the floor unconscious.

They carried me to the emergency room of the hospital where the doctors checked me over and told me that I was suffering from terrible nervous exhaustion and that my heart was 70 years old. From that time I began to tremble. I perspired and my heart palpitated up to 200. I could hardly breathe. Then I began to lose my memory. I could not even remember the names of my children — let alone memorize the Scriptures.

Still I kept insisting on preaching and I was carried to my platform. I preached eight minutes that first time before I fell down again. The next Thursday I preached five minutes before I fell. I knew that I couldn't continue my ministry like that.

Oh, the pain! If you don't have that experience of nervous frustration, you can't understand. Outwardly you look normal, but inwardly you are torn into pieces and you die every moment. The suffering is enormous. It is awful. I began crying to the Lord. I was not walking, I was lumbering. When I went to a place where many people were gathered together, my mind was shattered. I said, "Oh, God, what can I do? What can I do?"

Then I started to read Scriptures and while I was reading Acts, God began to give me a new revelation. Acts says that 3,000 people got saved on the first day; 5,000 on the second and then a multitude of people began to come. At that time they were using the temple of God as a meeting place.

While I was reading the Bible I realized they were involved in two types of ministry. They were gathering together in the temple, but on the other hand they were having meetings from house to house. They were mainly carrying out a teaching ministry and communion from house to house. In the temple gathering they were praying and sharing praise together, so they were having house-to-house ministry as well as temple ministry. I said, "What does this mean?" I'd only had a temple ministry. I only asked people to come to the temple. But what did "house-to-house" ministry mean? They were teaching the apostolic doctrine and they were sharing and breaking the bread from house-to-house and people were being added to their crowd.

I said, "I've never practiced this house-to-house ministry." But as I kept on reading, I began to see that they were having church in Aquilla and Priscilla's house, also in Lydia's house. I said, "What! Church in the home?"

Then the revelation poured into my mind and I sought God, asking: "Why can't I start this house-to-house ministry?" Since I couldn't carry out my normal ministry, why not let the deacon or deaconess become the leader and let them share the Word of God, teach them apostolic doctrine and break the bread together and share the love of God and let them come just on Sunday to praise God in the church?

I called all my deacons together and I was so excited as I explained to them, "You see how Moses tried to solve all the problems, but his father-in-law came and told him he should divide into 1,000 and 500 and 100 to take care or those things. This is the Word of God. We've been having temporal ministry, but as I read the Bible I realized they were having house-to-house ministry.

"Who do you think carried that ministry? There were only 12 apostles. There were only seven deacons, so they could never take care of tens of thousands of Christians. And so, I began to see clearly that a leading lay Christian had carried out this house-to-house ministry. I thought, "I should do this again in our church."

One by one my deacons began to agree with their pastor, but they said, "This is a new idea. We are afraid." They also added, "We need our privacy. We are working, so we need our privacy. We can't open our homes. We're not trained to do that. More than anything, you are picked to do that, and we are not paid. So, pastor, we can't do that. Don't try to put the responsibility on our shoulders. Why don't you go on a long vacation?" *That meant, "Why don't you resign?"* They were telling me nicely.

When they left I said, "God, this is a beautiful idea, but my deacons won't buy it. I'm lost."

Then the Spirit said, "Wait a minute, Why did you only try the deacons? Why don't you try the deaconesses?"

I cried, "Deaconesses! You mean I divide the whole church and delegate the deaconesses to take care of it?"

In Korea for 5,000 years the women didn't have any voice. I thought if I ever let the deaconesses take over and be in places of responsibility, I would be in a worse situation.

Then I kept praying and the Spirit got hold of me. If the Spirit gets hold, you cannot escape. You only think of it. While I was talking to myself, the Spirit was talking to me, "From whom was Jesus Christ born?" Woman! "On whose lap was He nurtured?" Woman! "Who surrounded His earthly ministry and supplied all His needs and helped Him?" Women! "Who appeared first when He was resurrected?" Women! "To whom did He give the first resurrection message to relate to the disciples?" Woman.

The Spirit said, "To my questions you have been answering one word only — woman. If I'm not afraid of using women — why are you afraid?"

That was the final thought He put in my mind, so I thought: "I'll try." I began by calling together the women leaders. When I explained the plan, I became amazed when they began to cry. They said, "We did not know you had such a struggle in your heart. We will carry the burden together with you."

They were entirely different from men. For that I praise God! They said, "We'll do anything whatsoever you ask us to do." So I bypassed the men and organized my whole church and delegated the women to go house-to-house. I appointed them as heads. Many women came with scratched faces and broken arms because their husbands beat them and men resisted when the untrained women tried to lay hands on them and pray for them. There was all sorts of trouble.

"My God!" I cried when all the deacons came to me and said they were going to leave the church. "Father," I wailed, "now I am in a desperate situation."

Then the Spirit said, "Don't worry. All good things come out of chaos."

The ladies began to do a marvelous job and I began to learn from them. They said, "Oh, pastor, publicly tell the people that you are delegating your authority to us because we are acting by ourselves so men do not respect us. Please delegate your authority to us and also let us carry out your message. We will write down your message for our Bible study because some of the women invent the craziest messages we have ever heard. Teach us how to conduct cell meetings."

And so, I wrote out their materials and taught them and then delegated my authority to them. You can read about my successful cell meetings in my book, The Fourth Dimension.

Then all the church settled down and unbelievers were added to my church. Then, by and by, men started to see the merits of the cell system and they also began to organize cells. They also came together. Right now I have more than 20,000 cell leaders who are unpaid assistants — housewives, technicians, lawyers and professors who are giving one afternoon a week according to their convenience to lead the cell system. They are doing marvelously well.

Read Ephesians 4:11-13 and, of course you'll know that God raised up prophets, evangelists, pastors and lay people so that they might carry out the ministry to the Body of Jesus Christ. Ministers are not supposed to carry out all the functions of the church, they are to teach the lay persons so they can carry out the ministry to the Body of Jesus Christ.

That part has been neglected. We have been afraid of delegating our authority to lay persons and that has been the reason most ministers are carrying such a load as the church grows bigger and bigger. A pastor is like an upside-down pyramid when he carries the whole burden. He becomes flat and dies very early. But when the ministry is delegated through the cell system, the minister sits on the top, and as the foundation becomes bigger and wider, the church is in a safer place.

Many people come to me and say, "Cho, you have half-a-million members. What a burden you carry!" Inside my heart, I laugh. I am sitting on top — the larger my church grows, the safer foundation I have. I don't carry so much of a burden.

In fact, I organized my church in such a way that I lost my job! In Korea when I come to church and to my office — I just receive a report from my leaders. Most of the counseling is taken care of on the cell level, through my associates.

I have not so much to do. I study some. When I have a good friend, I go out to play golf. Since I don't have so much work to do, I go out of my country six months out of 12 — going around the world preaching the Gospel.

Wherever I am — believe it or not — people are coming and packing out the place. In Korea, my associates tell me they have as many crowds as I have; when I show up there is no less — yet they have the same crowds. Of course, people are already well-fed, and have shared and fellowshipped in the cell system.

They come to church, not to hear any spectacular message (of course I try to preach a spectacular one), but they come to have the fellowship and the praise service in song and to celebrate the resurrection of Jesus Christ. Therefore, I am expendable. And I am so pleased, for most churches are built on personality. When I go to Europe there are so many cathedrals empty. They say, "When we had Dr. so-and-so this places was packed, but the place has been empty since he left." We must build the church on the Christian, not on a specific person, so the church might remain strong should that person leave.

We are expendable!

That's why our church is built on people ministering to people — not ministers doing everything!

You need to get to work in your church
(Stretch out your faith muscles!)

Lay minstry is important. Many a lay person is coming and sitting like a sitting duck, hearing with a deaf ear. It is no good! A church should get involved in a practical ministry by having the cell system. You will see a certain percentage of people are really involved, but a large portion of people are just participating in a service every Sunday as they come to observe how the ritualism is carried out.

But the more people who get involved in direct ministry, the greater success you can have. Suddenly we had involved people, not just observers. What percentage of your church is directly involved in ministry? The cell system is the way. Through it they divide into five or 10 families that once a week get together for no more than an hour.

They worship the Lord in song and in prayer. They share the Word and really pray for each other. They testify to each other. They also have sharing. During this Depression many people lost their jobs, but outsiders watch and say, "Oh, Lord, look at them — how they love each other," because each cell unit begins to bring rice and money and clothes. When they gather together for a cell meeting it is a law in my church that they bring extra clothes, rice, even cookies and money and anything extra they can to share with the unfortunate members. During a period of depression we have no trouble in our church. Although many of our people may lose their jobs, they will still have food, clothing and money to send their children to school because we are sharing.

Whatever is left from the cell groups they bring to church and our warehouse has a mountain of clothes and utensils and TV sets and bicycles and things like that. We are sharing the way people did in New Testament times. They shared with each other. This is a real expression of love and you can do it only through a cell unit because you know each other. The cell system is not only for sharing the Word of God and praying. The members really carry the burden for each other. If someone gets sick, some cell member will go clean the home and cook the meals. If someone dies, each member of the cell group will spend one evening with the family during the time of the funeral, really helping them!

Once they belong to a cell, they don't like to leave because it is a fantastic sharing group and an evangelistic outreach through which they touch their neighbors. If people are only gathering according to the heterogenous group — when you try to get lawyers together with butchers — they have no common language. Even in America, although they speak the same language, when you put together a lawyer and a butcher — they are foreigners to each other. When I first organized my cell system, I tried to mix them up. I'm not a segregationalist! I tried to put together lawyers and merchants, but they were foreign to each other. They were both Korean, but they were speaking entirely different languages, so they couldn't work well together.

By and by I started to know the situation so I reorganized the cell systems in homogenous groupings — lawyer cell systems, professor cell systems, I even made a banker cell system because bankers speak the same language. Through the homogenous groups they touch each other so freely and so easily. Heterogenous groups didn't do very much.

Also, the church membership had become so big and so vast that they could only have face-to-face fellowship. Then they come to the cell system, they can have heart-to-heart fellowship. In church they only had large numbers, but when they come to the cell groups they are called by their first names and they are treated like human beings.

To have a successful cell system, you must have vast logistics. You must have a training program. You don't appoint leaders at random. When you have a new cell, you soon appoint an assistant cell leader who needs to learn along with the main cell leaders.

The assistant must choose the proper time to attend our training course. In our church we have Lay Christians' Bible School, Lay Christians' Bible College and the Lay Christians' Graduate Course for terms of six months to one year, but we are operating the schools both day and night. If they have free time in the day, they can come then. If they have free time in the evening, they can come then. On Sunday we operate the school for the entire day and they can choose the Sunday course so all cell leaders are accredited graduates of Bible school, Bible college and Bible graduate school and they are almost all better-educated than standard Bible School graduates.

I constantly trained and recruited them and supplied the material so we now publish the material for a whole year. Once they get that cell leader's material, then we provide them with a weekly bulletin on which we have written our lessons so that they have the materials. Next, they need to be

motivated. Even though you get them organized — or you
don't motivate them — they are not going to move.

The only way to motivate them is to give
them clear-cut goals. If they don't have a goal, they lose their
sense of direction, so I ask them (I never force them but I
always ask them), "Each cell leader, please do your best to
lead one family to church every six months so that you lead
two families in a year." Then, between five and ten families
(when they concentrate with that goal to pray and help and
love) find it is easy to lead one new family to church. One
family usually consists of three to five members. If they gain
three members in six months, then each cell is going to lead
six people. Multiply that by 20,000 and you get 120,000 new
members without any fanfare.

Our evangelistic outreach program is very solid. Hundreds
of new souls are streaming into church every week because
we give them quotas and they pray. Some people are against
having quotas, but if they had none, the the people who ob-
ject would never work. If you ask the mountain climbers to
go and climb the mountain, they would never climb it, but if
you showed them the peak, then they would climb. Given a
specific goal, the cell leaders will have a sense of direction,
they will be motivated and they will always ascertain for
themselves if they are arriving at their goals or not. When
they have brainstorming sessions, then give them abundant
praise. Build up their self-image . "You did it! Beautiful!"

Through that, you can plan for next year's growth. One
gentleman and his wife came to my office and said, "Pastor, I
want to register as a member of this church, but listen to our
story. We were not Christians. We were living in one area
and our son had become a hippie — long hair, guitar, all kinds
of crazy pictures on the wall. He wouldn't go to school. He
had us terribly worried. We did everything, but he wouldn't
change his life-style .

"There was a beautiful lady living close to us. She had a tremendous smile and she started to visit my son and they became friends. She just accepted him as he was. He began to visit her home and suddenly changed. He cut his hair and took down all those crazy things. Instead of them, he put up pictures of Jesus Christ. He became a clean-cut, beautiful young person.

"Then the lady invited me and my wife to her home. She said she was having a religious meeting with tea and coffee and an ashtray. She told me I could smoke. I was a great smoker and was afraid of attending a religious service, but since she said she had an ashtray, my wife and I went.

"Sure enough, there were other smokers. We enjoyed cookies and tea and we heard about religion and Jesus Christ. What a wonderful love those people had! We heard a beautiful testimony explaining the Word of God and we enjoyed the evening thoroughly."

"The next Friday she invited us again, so we went. For a couple of months we attended and went from house to house on Fridays and we enjoyed it and were quite indoctrinated. Then she told us that on the next Sunday we had a preengagement and we were going to the mother church where thay had a wonderful pastor who would give a tremendous lecture."

"Out of appreciation, my wife and I went and I was impressed with the magnitude of the church and you gave a beautiful message. I was impressed with that, but I did not enjoy the atmosphere."

My church is enthusiastic. You can imagine how we were clapping hands and praising God! He declared, "They were all a bunch of crazy people! I told my wife that I enjoyed the sermon, but I didn't enjoy the atmosphere and I would not go there anymore. Determined not to return, we went home, but the next Friday the lady with the smile invited us to

another home and then she told us that she was going to wait
in her car in front of such and such a gate for us to go to Sunday
services. We tried every kind of excuse, but she would not
budge. She said we had to go to church. On Sunday she came
and she was honking.

"We went, but we disliked the atmosphere even more. We
felt bound by her. She was such a wonderful lady and we
couldn't deny her invitation.

"We decided to move out of town —
secretly. We called the realtor and we sold our home and very
secretly we moved out into another area. When we moved,
we thought: Wonderful! We are free now! But the lady cell
leader went to the town hall and found out our new address
as soon as she learned that we had moved."

The cell leader jotted down the people's new address and
turned it into our ministry department which is appointed
for each cell system in each district. The address was sorted
out and given to the cell leader in the area into which they
had moved. So, they told me for one week, they were happy
because they had no visitation from a Christian, but the next
week they heard a knock at the door.

The man told.me, "We went to the door and there stood a
dozen people with a bouquet and cookies and cried,
"Welcome!"

"Then I asked, 'Who are you?' They answered, 'We are
the cell leaders of this area. You belong to us now. You are
transferred from the other area to our area.' Without getting
permission, they came into the room. They decorated with
flowers, took out the cookies and they had services."

The man told me that after they left, he and his wife sat
there almost crying. They said that they would never be able
to leave the church. If they wanted to, they would either have
to move to America or to heaven. Otherwise they felt they
would never be allowed to leave the church. So, lacking any

alternative, they told me they had decided to become full-fledged members.

They did and later they even took offices and they themselves are now cell leaders!

That is why so many churches aren't growing: they not only open the front door, but they open the back door very wide. You may have new members coming in the front door, but so many are slipping out the back door that soon you realize there is no increase. Open the front door wide — and shut the back door. How can you do that? Through the cobwebs of the elaborate cell system.

One lady tried to resign from my church .

In order to resign from my church, a member must go over five hurdles, his cell leader, then a licensed associate, then an ordained minister, then my personal associate, then me. The woman who wanted to resign was determined to pass successfully over all the hurdles, but when her name came to me, I called her by telephone. She was very cold and said, "I am determined to leave, pastor."

I said, "OK, but at least I want to meet with you." And so, I made arrangements. I asked the service department how much she had paid tithes, offerings and the construction fund. When I gathered all the material, I found it amounted to several tens of thousands of dollars.

When I met her, I said: "You have successfully passed through all the hurdles."

She laughed and I laughed. "I'm going to pass through your hurdle, too," she said.

"OK, but remember this one thing: you are leaving my church, but you don't know how much money you are leaving. You are leaving an investment in my church that almost equals your lifetime savings." I showed her all the totals of the offerings she had given to the church. I said, "You gave this much to this church so you and your children are bound to this church. You have such a large investment in it. Do you still want to give it all up in such a way?"

She looked at the figures and said, "My, I did not know I gave so much."

I prayed for her, then I left. After a few days she called again and said, "I have decided to stay here."

She did not pass through my hurdle.

It is one thing to gather people together, yet another to keep them there. People are not usually leaving the church because of the poor sermons — people are leaving because of the lack of love. People are dying for love. If you properly share love with them, they are going to stay even though they hear very poor sermons.

How can you supply that love? Through the cobweb of the love of the cell system. When you get many cell systems, you can't really attend to the individual's needs, so you must get organized.

One couple came to me and said they were going to Inchon which is about a 40-minute drive on the freeway. They told me they had come to say good-bye.

I said, "OK. Go, but find a good fundamental church to attend."

They answered, "But, pastor, we want to still attend the mother church. We will go and set up the cell system. Since we cannot come on Wednesday, we will set up the cell system to meet then."

I was nonchalant and said, "OK. God bless you."

After a couple of years they came and asked, "Pastor, would you come to our area and bless us?"

I said, "You know I am a very busy person. I can't visit each home personally. If I set out to visit a home every day, it would take more than 70 years to make an every-member visitation."

They said, "Oh, no, pastor. We do not want you to visit our home. We want you to come visit our cell."

I said, "Your cell would be five to ten families. Why should I spend time? I am busy."

They answered, "For the past two years we have been having cell-splitting and cell-splitting and cell-splitting. You guess how many we have."

I asked, "two hundred?"

"Two thousand!"

When I went there, I spoke at a hall that was packed with people — people who were there because this one couple began to multiply and multiply through the cell system until they reached 2,000!

I held a wonderful church service and then I sent one of my associates there. Last year the membership ran up to 5,000 — because of one couple!

In Korea now we have many high-rise apartments because Korea is a small country similar to Florida. The world is very evil so there are many muggers and people are afraid. When you knock at the door, they greet you through a peek hole and ask, "Who are you?"

"Christian."

Often that does not touch them and therefore many people were out of reach. We were all worried, but one wonderful lady, a cell leader, volunteered to sell her house and move into an apartment dwelling. She began to fill every floor with our cell system so we invited her to give a lecture. The cell leaders and I went to hear her. She said she had been praying to find a way for God to lead her into knowing other people in the apartment house. She asked Him, "How can I touch them? They are behind closed doors!"

Then the Spirit spoke to her, "Through what way do they go to their home every day?"

She said, "Elevator!"

The Spirit said, "Turn the elevator into your chapel."

From then on, every Saturday she would stay on the elevator for three hours — going up and down, up and down with a big smile and she would make friends with people — carrying groceries for older folks and children for the younger ones. She would say, "I live here in the apartments on such-and-such a floor. Where do you live?"

One by one they began to come and she started to win them over to Jesus Christ. After her lecture, I asked the cell leaders to donate two or three hours every Saturday. Now, if you go to any apartment house in Seoul, Korea, you will find the smiling cell leader riding up and down, up and down. The apartment houses are filled with our cell system. Where there's a will, there's a way!

Right now our church is not the big cement building. That is just the celebration hall. Really, my church is in the apartment house, in the town, in the village, in the army bunker, the marketplace, the school.

We have children's cells. About 15,000 come on Sundays, but there are 70,000 children in Sunday school in the cell system. We have the children's cell system, youth cell system and the college system. We organize cells in every college and university. They have services there and that helps me very much because I don't have to spend more money to enlarge my space. There is endless growth!

The best way to lead people to Jesus Christ is through their neighbors. At this time many are afraid to speak to unknown people. They are very much afraid and scared, but neighbors know each other. They might not like to come to church, but they can go to their friend's house and easily become converted.

Faith will help you survive anything

(Even if the Communists are only a few miles away

In Korea we are constantly under the intimidation of communistic invasion. They may come down and destroy the mother church, and kill all the ministers, but the next moment the church will go underground.

If the Communists attack, there will be no time. The distance between Seoul and the Communists is the same as from downtown Washington, D.C., to Washington's Dulles Airport. Think of that! Can you imagine being downtown and having the enemy as close as the airport? We are in that situation!

If they attack, we will have no time. It would only take two minutes by airplane to attack Korea. Seoul will be right on the front line. When the war breaks, it happens. It will take less than one hour, if the armored soldiers rush to Seoul.

Because of this we are all prepared. In a radio message I have ready, I say: "Cell leaders, now this is an emergency. I have no time to meet you on Sunday. Listen to instructions. You will not find your pastors in church anymore, but I give you instructions. Go underground. Take good care of your people. Farewell. I will be waiting for you in heaven."

That's my message. It's all recorded in a station. Any time the Communists attack, we'll release this radio and TV announcement. I always give instruction to the workers in my church — as soon as the first bullet comes, burn up all the records.

I know I am the first target for the Communists. When they come, I will be killed. All the leaders and the church building will be destroyed, but they will never destroy our church because the vast movement will go underground. Who can round up 20,000 people? Nobody!

Our Christians will not be left shepherdless. They'll have a shepherd underground. I'm carrying out evangelism in Red China. Right now my workers in evangelism are visiting China. They visit house to house; cell system to cell system. I can't name them — it would be very dangerous to do so.

In China there are between 15 million and 100 million Christians underground at present through the cell system. Ninety percent of the cell leaders are women under 40 years of age who have never seen the Christian church or missionaries in their entire lives. You might think that China under communism has blotted out all Christianity, but all through their reign of terror the Holy Spirit has been working among the people. That is the country where the Holy Spirit Himself organized the cell system and cells sometimes consist of 500 people.

They have healings and conversions. Many communistic leaders come in secret in the night to get healed because they don't have proper medication. They bring their families to the cell system and they get healed. So many leading Communists are secret Christians there.

The members work in the field or factory. After they come home about twelve o'clock at night, they hold a service which lasts from one to two o'clock in the cell system. Most of the leaders are women and they are doing marvelously well. I'm supplying the materials through my radio broadcasts. They write them down as they listen to the radio station, and they use the materials. In that kind of situation, the cell system is the only way. Lay Christians are a tremendous asset to the kingdom of God for carrying out the ministry.

For successfully carrying out the cell system, you need Paul's ministry, Peter's ministry and John's ministry because Paul was called into the ministry while he was building tents. The church is like a tent. You need the mother church ministry. You can't get rid of the mother church in the cell system.

You also need Peter's ministry. Peter was called while he was casting nets. The cell system is a net. Too difficult to win them without the cell system! One by one they come without the cell system, but when you cast a net and pull, you are going to catch 100-150 fish.

Through the cell system you can draw a big number of souls. That is Peter's ministry, but John was called while he was mending the nets and that is why you need a lot of associates. The associates are called to mend the broken cell system. Sometimes a cell leader dies or one defects, then you need to appoint your associate over the broken group to mend the broken net. If you have that kind of ministry, then you can keep the cells growing constantly as long as you have associates that can go and mend the cells and make them strong again.

You just need to cast the net and gather the fish. Once they go through the cell, there will be no way for them to back-slide. They are brought to church. In my experience I found that we had to pull them to church at least four times. Even though the new member was converted publicly, he needed to be taken to the church service a minimum of four times before he came by himself.

There is a reason why we lose so many people after they have made a public decision. When Billy Graham came to

Korea, we had a wonderful service. Thirty thousand made decisions and our church received 100 decision cards. We began to visit them through the cell system. Amazingly, less than ten percent of them volunteered to come to church. Most of them said, "We just went out to see Billy Graham because he was so close. We came out that day because we felt like that, but don't visit us now."

A public meeting at this place, can give a shock or a real presence of the church to a whole unbelieving society, but the most effective way is to get them to come by a personal touch. Personal soul-winning is still the way to go forward. Who will bring a sinner to the church more than four times? If you don't belong to a cell, no one is eager enough to do that. But when the cell leaders say, "You take that lady," or "You take that man," you will take him more that four times to church. You often pay his taxi fare, buy his lunch, everything! Then he settles down in our church.

To make it effective you need John's ministry, Peter's ministry of casting the net and you need Paul's ministry to gather them together under the heavenly tent and feed them. Then you will have a growing church. There will be no plateau where you stop. You will see lots of souls saved.

You can have a very successful church in this way. You will have many laborers and abundant finances and you will be able to carry out world missions very easily. Without enough workers, enough finances — how can you carry out world mission through radio, TV, literature, seminars and every other way? I'm trying to win over the Japanese for Jesus Christ. In Korea I have a strong foundation with my TV ministry, my seminars, my crusades and literature compaigns so we are sweeping Japan because we have a strong home foundation. If you don't have a strong foundation as logistics stand, you cannot carry out world missions as I have a strong church and have real visions and dreams in my heart. Sooner or later you will see a church spring up with hundreds of thousands of members if you will learn how to multiply your ministry through lay Christians. Who wouldn't have revival with 20,000 unpaid associates? They would be fools then if they couldn't have revival.

If you could only learn this principle, then you will multiply your ministry by 10,000, 20,000 and you will have a church of 100,000, 200,000. You will have enough workers and finances then to shake your city and your town. Lift up your head like Abraham and look to the north and south and east and west and claim your cities and your nations for the sake of Jesus Christ. The only hope for this generation is in Jesus Christ. When you get all of your nation saved and when they pay their taxes all honestly then you will not have your national debt problem! That is essential, you know.

To me, the problem is very simple. You cannot solve it by politics, you can solve it only by evangelism. When the citizens become honest and quit looking for loopholes in their taxes, in a couple of years you will be able to pay off the national debt.

The problem here is evangelism. Your ministries are genuinely patriotic and you can help solve this national problem. No other sinners can bring a solution to this problem. If America cannot solve this problem soon — then doomsday is coming. It is approaching very fast right now. America already has two strikes against it, and the last strike is coming very fast.

That is the reason why I have mobilized all my Christians to desperately pray for America.

I know the situation and it is serious — no joke! All the political people cannot solve the problem because they need the votes. Only the Christian can help the situation, so it is my heart's desire that you will rise up and meet the challenge and write a new history for America.

Chapter 15

Dr. Thomas F. "Tommy" Reid

Yes, prayer will work for you, too

(Remember, you're not talking to yourself!)

We Christians pray very little. Sad to say, that is mainly because we tend to make prayer a one-way street.

At its best, a one-way conversation is extremely boring. I've had the experience of going to the airport (perhaps you have, too) to pick up a well-known speaker. I had decided to go myself to get him rather than have a staff person pick him up — only to find that he didn't talk. On our way back, I would attempt to make conversation only to be answered with a "yep" — a grunt — or a "no" — followed by complete silence. By the time we reached the motel, I was extremely happy to drop him off. I had waited a lifetime to meet this celebrity — only to find out that he didn't talk.

It's interesting that Paul closes 2 Corinthians with the words, "the communion" of the Holy Spirit. It is impossible to have communion without some form of articulation.

I would like to propose to you some helps that I have found in my own life. I have been to Korea and have seen them pray and one of the questions that is often asked of me, because people know I sometimes travel with Dr. Cho is: "Is it cultural — are cell groups culturally Korean?"

I've been able to say, "No, they're not because I've seen them work in our church." I started cell groups and now have some 240 groups and found they work in America and they are not simply culturally Korean.

Nor is prayer! Interestingly enough — communication with God is not just Korean!

Some of the things Dr. Cho has said to me and to his audiences across the world have caused me to evaluate what prayer is. Is it a two-way conversation? If it is — then it should not be a boring experience! I keep hearing about prayer being difficult work and I know sometimes intercession can be difficult. But then I wonder if we really understand what prayer is, because I have never had communion with somebody (and that's even deeper than fellowship) be boring. It is not boring to be around someone we enjoy or like.

When we pray, we should not just be saying, "I want you to bless so and so," but it is permitting God to speak to us about them — the communion of the Holy Spirit. It is God's utmost desire to talk with us!

Not only does God wish to speak with us concerning our day, but I believe God is trying to create within us the dimension of our life that He wants to bring to pass.

As Dr. Cho says in his book, *The Fourth Dimension*, this is the dimension of being able to envision things in the spiritual that God is trying to create in our lives. For example, Dr. Cho is no longer praying for a church of half a million. He is praying for a present church of 1 million members because that is the church that is already in his spirit.

I believe that is a principle that we find throughout the Scripture. Joseph, while he was in prison, prayed, not for his present circumstances, but in the vision that God had given him many years before in his homeland. What he saw was not his circumstance at the moment, he envisioned the dream, the destiny that God had created in his heart.

God is creating a new church — a body of believers in the fourth dimension in our hearts. It will not be of mortar and stone, but it will be in our hearts. It may not come to pass a month from now, a year from now. It may be two years from now — but God is attempting to create that vision in our hearts today.

In 1962, I was in the land of Korea, riding on a train in a private compartment with Dr. Cho. On our way between Seoul and some southern city in the tip of Korea, Dr. Cho and I talked. We'd become close personal friends. We were considering the possibility of my staying with him the rest of my life as a missionary in Korea and working with him in building his dream of a great Korean church.

Just as though a lightning bolt from heaven hit, God said to me, "This is not your place. I do not want you in Korea." I'd come to love Korea and to a certain extent my heart was there, but then the Lord said to me, "I want you to go back to your home city in Buffalo, N.Y. There I want you to build a church."

I looked at my Korean brother, who was talking as all this was churning inside of me, then I said, "Brother Cho, I cannot stay with you. I have a feeling that God is speaking into my spirit right now. I have to go back to my home."

We left it there and went on to a little city called Chung Ju to a Presbyterian church. One morning I awakened early and went to the platform for one of those five o'clock prayer meetings. I sat beside Dr. Cho and some others as an elderly Korean pastor led the worship. He was almost gliding across the platform and the people were raising their hands and praising the Lord and I shook my head and declared, "These can't be Presbyterians!" — but they were!

All of a sudden, something happened to me. Those

people disappeared and in their place I saw literally thousands of American faces. I noticed that a Catholic priest was leading the worship of all those Americans and God said to me, "Tommy, if you go back to Buffalo, I will do more for you than I have ever done in Korea. This which you see in your vision is the church I will create."

I came back to Buffalo and in times of discouragement I felt like Joseph when he sat in the prison. I felt for seven years that I was in a prison.

There came a point in my ministry when I said, "God, if You don't do something for me soon, I'm going to give up. I don't understand why years ago You gave me that dream. That vision was so direct that I will never forget it — and here I am, sitting with problems and no success and hardly any people! Why am I here?"

Every time I got down to the very depths, my dream was renewed. God kept saying to me, "When you pray — don't pray for your church in the natural — pray for the church you saw in your dream."

If you have read my book, you might recall the story of how God sent a Catholic priest into my life. I'd always had a hard time with Catholic theology, but when we learned to know each other, I invited that precious man of God into my home. He lived with us for almost a year and got up every morning and went to mass.

I watched as part of my dream was fulfilled when that man led our people in worship. The church began to grow and suddenly I realized that when God gives a vision — when God gives a dream — if we have faith, it will come to pass.

One of the most exciting things about prayer is that God does creative work in our hearts. He puts a seed down in our spirits. I do not think there is a Christian leader who God hasn't told, "This is what I want you to do in your ministry. This is something that I'm creating." God may be creating a vision in your mind right now. Looking at your ministry — your life at the present time — it may not be the way you see it with your spiritual eyes. It can be so different that it can be almost the antithesis. But you know as clearly as you know where you are sitting at this moment, it is even more real than what you have in the natural.

That's prayer! It's not a boring adventure, but an exciting experience when we come into the reality of the creativity of God. I like to go to the mirror in the morning when I get up and say to my image, "Tommy Reid, in the natural, you may not be very important in this world. But today, despite the problems you face, the creativity of the Holy Spirit lies within you and by faith you are creative this day. God, by the Holy Spirit, places an unquenchable dream within you and it is prayer that makes it birth into reality."

That's what Dr. Cho talks about in his Fourth Dimension. It is not simply Korean. It is not something that just works there. It is something that works for every person no matter where you are. Every single person has experienced that dimension in his heart.

No matter how big a thing God has put in our hearts, He has made it even bigger than when it started. I'm trying to tell you that prayer is the most exciting thing in the world! It's the only thing that can change the world. It's not a matter of getting down and ordering him, "God, change the world, God, do this or that."

"Lord, help me to be involved in Your plan," is all I have to say and then God drops a great big bomb inside my spirit. He simply says, "What you are praying about, I'm going to do it through you!" Notice those words that make the difference in your prayer life: "The communion of the Holy Spirit."

Most of you wrestle about the time you spend in prayer. Dr. Cho spends four hours a day praying, so you try to make a mathematical tabulation on how you could work that into your schedule. But may I propose to you something even greater than that?

The communion of the Holy Spirit! It's not just a matter of blocking out time for God, it is a matter of living in His presence, of having consistent communion with Him, of knowing as we drive the car or fly in the plane or visit a hospital that God is with us through the communion of the Holy Spirit.

One thing is necessary to help with your prayer journal when you take it with you into your prayer closet and into God's presence. God said to John on the island of Patmos, "Write it down." The Old Testament prophet said, "Write it down." I say to you, write what the Holy Spirit reveals to you down beside the thing you are praying about in your prayer journal.

When God first began to speak to us about having cell groups — the concept was born in prayer. The more I thought about it, the more I knew that this was God's plan for the church. But a lot of us read or hear about such things and, even though we are inspired, decide: "Yes, I heard the logistics and I'm going to share this with my church and we're going to start mushrooming from two to four to eight to 16 to 32 groups and we're going to take off like lightning and we're going to have a great church."

You start off. When you reach the 15th group, one of the leaders goes off and begins a new church. And this devastates you! You block out what the Lord has said about cell groups and declare that you no longer think the concept is for your church.

I don't know if cell groups are the way you should go or not, but I do know that God spoke to me and told me to do it. I was riding along in my car one day, listening to a tape from a series. As I took in the message, God dropped a seed into my heart.

He said, "Tommy, when you say the word church — what does it mean? What do you see?"

"I see a steeple and a building and people sitting in pews," I responded.

God spoke, "That's not the church."

I said, "Yes, Lord, I know. The church is people."

All of a sudden, a dream was born in my heart and it was this: I came to a place where that when I heard or said the word church, I no longer saw the steeple and the people in the pews, but people in the factories bowing in prayer, gathering in homes to minister to the sick, our people — no matter where they are — being the church out in the world on Monday, Tuesday, Wednesday, Thursday and Friday. After that, when I said the word church that's what I saw!

And so, I took my prayer journal out and put the word church on it and then I put down the structure that we now have: pastor, assistant pastors, district leaders and branch churches and the cell groups. I put down homes and factories for people worshiping there. I wrote down the offices and so forth. Then I said, "Lord, help me to see the church like that," and for several years I prayed in that vision. We did not make a concentrated effort toward cell groups until I could honestly stand and say, "When I say the word church, this is what I see."

It was birthed like a seed, but it grew to a dream when I prayed in the dream. Through this writing, God is planting a seed in your heart — whatever it may be. When that seed is watered by prayer, it turns into a vision and what you've seen in your spirit turns into a vision and what you see in your vision is greater than what you actually see in the flesh. It's faith that transfers it from the spirit into the flesh — the actual.

We can talk about all the systems of growth we want to talk about, but the basic foundation is that kind of envisioning prayer that says to you, "Yes, I know that God has spoken to me. I absolutely know that God has put a seed in my heart." Then we go into our prayer closet, drive the car, fly in a plane and we experience the communion of the Holy Spirit.

When we eat dinner, even when we lie in our beds, we put that vision up before us. Our mates might think we're crazy, but we take our diagrams and put them beside us and say, "That's what I see myself (or my church) becoming." After the seed, the watering. Someday — perhaps sooner than you realize — God will give birth to the dream.

I admit to you that prayer was boring to me. I was brought up in a Pentecostal home. I knew what the fellowship of the Holy Spirit was. I knew how it was to be blessed. I knew all those things, but one day it occurred to me that God wanted to be a consistent conversationalist with me! And that is an exciting dimension as we pray in our dream and the seed turns into a vision and the vision turns into reality — the process that must take place because we are the church and the church is born of the spirit. If you want to be holy, the Holy Spirit has to build your dreams in your heart.

One of my businessman friends has made hundreds of millions of dollars. He tells me that the way you make money is not in your head. He claims, "Every time I've had a business born in my head, it has been either a mundane success or a total failure. But when I've been out relaxing," and he specifically likes to quote Psalm 23, "as I speak God's Word in a relaxed method, all of a sudden, I get an idea from the depths of my being, and out of the spirit comes the ideas of God."

That's what I'm trying to convey. No one wants you to put this down and say, "I'm such a miserable failure. I don't know how to pray." Instead, it's a matter of deciding, "I'm going to enter into the most exciting dimension of my life — into a dimension having communion with the Holy Spirit."

Chapter 16
Dr. Robert Schuller

How to strengthen your faith

(You may have to start a church in a drive-in!)

I hope and pray that what I share here will be just a simple witness — not a sermon, but a testimony. To tell you the truth, I don't like to think of myself as someone who bears witness. I say that a preacher is a spokesman for God, exposing the truth of His Word to God's people and if you are a pastor talking to the redeemed folk of God, then it is appropriate that you deliver a sermon, probably from a pulpit.

But what would you do if you started a church from scratch with only your wife as a member, which was the case with me 29 years ago; if, at your opening service, the only people who showed up were non-Christians?

Now that's an interesting experience, and that's where I'm coming from, for it was 30 years ago in February that I received a call from the Reformed Church in America to go to California to begin a new mission and a new church. They were Dutch people and the Dutch are known to be thrifty. That's the positive word. Another word might be "tight."

A favorite story of mine illustrates a profound principle of biblical faith, or what I call "possibility thinking." The reason I use the term "possibility thinking" instead of faith is because I talk to a lot of people who aren't prepared to accept the Bible as the Word of God, and I'm not about to quote a source that they don't respect.

After all, I see my role as an evangelist leading people into a personal relationship with Jesus Christ until they know Him as a personal Savior and are filled with His Holy Spirit and His love.

I'm not primarily someone who is trying to get people to be worshipers of every verse in the sacred Scriptures, which I do accept as the Word of God, but I think the Bible is to lead us to a relationship with the Lord, and we're saved by the Blood, not by the Book. I think that Christ is Lord over the Scriptures and the Spirit gives life, but the letter has a way of dividing people.

So that's where I am.

To illustrate the principle of biblical faith, here is the story of the man who lived in Ridgewood, New Jersey, and bought a mobile home in Long Island. He illustrates what I call "possibility thinking," which means that he made the right decision before he solved the problem.

In good management you never surrender leadership to the problem. You don't bring the problem-solving phase into the decision-making phase. If you do, you've already surrendered leadership to problems instead of to possibilities.

Faith is making the right decisions simply because you know that this is what God wants you to do, even though you haven't the foggiest idea how you're going to get out of the mess that you're going to get into because you've made the decision. (If you waited until you had a solution to all the problems before you made the decision, my goodness, you'd never get married. Right? Can I be sure these children will all turn out OK?)

The fellow bought the mobile home in Long Island. He lived in Ridgewood, New Jersey. He made the decision. Now he has to solve the problem — which is how to get the trailer across Manhattan Island without getting it demolished by the wild, insane drivers.

Now the secret of success is simple: all you do is hire people smarter than you are. He went to a Manhattan cop and asked, "When's the best time to pull my mobile home across Long Island?"

The cop replied, "Simple. Sunday morning at 7 o'clock. All the Catholics are at Mass and if you can get the Catholics in New York off the streets, you've got a lot going for you. On top of that, all the Jews are on the golf course, and if you get the Catholics and the Jews off the streets, boy, the traffic really clears away. To top it off, the Protestants are all sleeping.

So the man followed the cop's advise and on Sunday morning at 7 o'clock he entered Manhattan Island. You could shoot a cannon down Fifth Avenue and not hit a thing.

All of a sudden he got rammed in the rear by a Seventh-Day Adventist late for work!

I've said that faith is making the right decision before you solve the problems. That is what faith is all about. You know, it wasn't until Moses heard the thunder and the puffs of the horses' of the chariots of Pharoah breathing down his neck that the waters parted in the Red Sea.

I was called 29 years ago to begin this new church in California. It was a call to a church with nothing. All I was given was $500. My wife was my only member. I had a daughter three years old, a son six months old. I wrote a friend in California, "I don't mind coming and starting a church from scratch, but please would you line up an empty hall so that when I come there I can conduct a church service?"

He wrote back — I'll never forget it — as if this were one of the primary lessons God was teaching me.

"It is impossible to find an empty hall in Garden Grove." For the first time in my life, that word impossible suddenly appeared as the most irresponsible, reckless, wild, extreme, stupid word I had ever heard in my life.

I had not been to Garden Grove, but I, from Chicago, could imagine that there might be some possible places and I did something that I'm sure was Spirit-directed. Driving to California, stopping at a cafe in Albuquerque, New Mexico, I impulsively, intuitively, took out a napkin and wrote down the numbers one to ten, not even knowing why I was doing it. Then I prayed secretly, "Lord, there has got to be a place." I thought of ten possible places to begin a church when my friend, an expert with his PhD., told me with certainty that there was "no possible place at all."

Ignoring that reckless, negative counsel, I began to write down out of my prayer thoughts the ten possibilities. Number one, we'll rent a school building. Number two, we'll rent the Masonic Hall. Number three, I think, was we'll rent a mortuary chapel. Number four, five, six, I forget what they were. The seventh, I remember: we'll rent the Seventh-Day Adventist Church. Number eight, we'll rent the Jewish Synagogue. Number nine, we'll use a drive-in theater. Number ten, we'll rent an acre of ground and pitch a tent. But don't tell me it's impossible.

When I got to California, I found out it was against the law to rent schools, so that was closed. There was no Masonic Hall. The Baptists were in the only mortuary chapel. (The best part is, they're still there!) I got to the Seventh-Day Adventist Church. There was one, and Tom Gillespie, a young Presbyterian pastor, had already nailed it down and was starting church services there. Incidentally, he is now the newly elected and installed president of Princeton Theological Seminary.

Finally in desperation, we went to a drive-in theater. I

asked if I could use it for a church service, and the man said, "What?"

I repeated the question and he said, "OK."

So we announced that we were going to have church services in the drive-in church starting Sunday, March 27, 1955.

We invited all people to come. Incidentally, I found about six Dutch Reformed families in town. I called on them thinking they would be the nucleus. But in our Reformed Church in America, we're not any different from most denominations with maybe the exception of the Assemblies of God and the totally positive Pentecostal denominations. In most denominations, including ours, I'd say half of the people are negative and half are positive. You know that Jesus Christ saves to the uttermost all those who believe in His name. It's possible to be born-again and go to heaven even if you've spent your whole life being a miserable, negative thinker.

I really think that's possible. It takes a lot of faith for me to say that and I may amend that when I think about it a little more.

At any rate, I found that these six Dutch Reformed people happened to be negative people with the exception of two couples and those two couples I urged to attend my new church.

The rest I encouraged to remain where they were because they were "doing such wonderful work and the Lord needed them."

I was afraid they'd come and bring their negative friends and negative relatives. There are churches that start that way, with a nucleus of negative people. Negative, cantankerous people. And they bring their negative relatives and friends.

Do you know what I really believe? The church of Jesus Christ is a divine institution. It's not a human institution. It is a divine institution made up of human beings, but it is a divine institution — the only institution that God ever placed upon Planet Earth and entrusted with the responsibility of perpetuating the truth of the Gospel from generation to generation. The church has to be a divine institution, simply for the fact that it survives. You think about it. We have been our own worst enemy.

Well, I started services on March 27, 1955, in the drive-in theater.

I started running ads in the paper.

I invited people to come to church. One of my denominational officials came to me on Saturday, March 19, 29 years ago, knocked at my door and said, "Bob Schuller, what do I hear? You're going to start a Reformed Church in a drive-in theater?"

"Well, that's the intention."

"How can you expect God to bless the preaching of the Gospel in that ... that ... that ..." he blushed as he said, "passion pit?"

"Well, you may be more of an authority on that than I am, but I'll tell you one thing. Paul preached on Mars Hill. You talk about pagan places!" When Paul took his missionary journeys, you stop and think about where he preached. It isn't where you preach, but what you deliver."

I rang doorbells, because I was desperate. About this time I had a sickening feeling. I thought I was going to California, start a new church, which would be a branch of the Reformed Church, and I would start off with about 20, 50, 100 good, solid, Dutch members and we'd be off and running. I found six families. Four were disqualified.

That left two couples. We had 200,000 members in the United States. I calculated that in 20 years, I'd be lucky if 100 Reformed Church people moved to our territory. If 80 of them were negative, I'd be in an awful mess.

Really depressed, I prayed about this. "Lord, why did I come out here anyway?"

Chapter 17
Dr. Robert Schuller

How to pray on four levels

(You may find yourself praising God like some sort of fanatic!)

"Ask and you shall receive. Seek and you shall find. You have not because you ask not," the Lord told us.

So, I ask for what I need.

You know, I'm a great believer in two-way prayer. I like to tell people that I pray on four levels. One is petition. That's when I ask God for something that's very selfish. That's perfectly fine. He tells us we can.

When I ask for what I need, that's petition. Intercession is next. That's when I pray for you. The third level of prayer is praise. And in praise, I discipline myself to begin every sentence with a "thank you," even though I haven't the foggiest notion what the rest of the sentence will be. The Holy Spirit always reminds me of something I should be grateful for, then the sentence always completes itself. I tell people that when you're really in a panic and the roof collapses and the walls fall in, and the unthinkable happens, then the only thing to do is to pray on that third level.

Forget petition.

Forget intercession.

Just start praising God, like I did when I was ministering with Paul Yonggi Cho in his church in Korea. I got the call that my daughter, Carol, was having her leg amputated in a Sioux City, Iowa, hospital. It nearly killed me. We got on a plane as quickly as possible. I remember Cho saying to me at the airport, praying, praying, and quoting Romans, *"All things work together for good to those who love God and keep his commandments. God will bless this."*

I preached that and believed it, but it was tough to take at a time like that. Coming across the ocean, I felt I couldn't hold back the bawling any longer. I'd been crying silent tears, but then I went to the lavatory, closed the door and started bawling. Boo-hoo bawling. I had only bawled once or twice. Before, all I could hear was Paul's people in the congregation in Seoul singing, "Hallelujah, hallelujah." The next thought the Lord gave me was, "Schuller, don't waste all this noise." So, I just changed my lips a bit, and my tongue, and verbalized the word Hallelujah. "Hallelujah ... Hallelujah ... HALLELUJAH ... Hallelujah ... Hallelujah ...."

The next time you bawl, don't waste the noise. Shape the word, "Hallelujah."

Praise!

Amazing how God blessed that, because out of that praise, "Hallelujah," came one of the greatest gifts God ever gave me. I think some of the greatest gifts God ever gives anybody are ideas. The gift was a sentence: "Schuller, play it down and pray it up! Believe that God will do something good out of it."

Well, that's prayer on the third level. Prayer on the highest level is where I've been living, I'd say, since the day I received the call to start the church 29 years ago. I've been living on what I call, "Prayer life on the fourth level." I call it two-way prayer. In two-way prayer, I discipline myself to ask questions only. I really clean up my prayer act; don't fill it up with a lot of sermonic material. I mean a lot of my prayers at times have had the inclination to be short sermons — telling God that the weather is nice. He already knows that. And God knows when I've got problems. He knows that before I am aware of it. On this level, all I do is ask questions.

The trick is to prepare for prayer by deciding what questions I want to ask the Almighty.

Ask questions.

Then be quiet and let the Holy Spirit write the answer in your mind, until you know that you know that you know that this is what you have to do.

That's guidance — Holy Spirit guidance.

It was on that level that I felt I was directed to start in at the drive-in theater. It was also on that level that I asked the questions, "God, what did I come out here for? There's a Presbyterian church, a Lutheran church, a Methodist church, an Assemblies of God church, a Holy Bible church, and an Open Bible church. You name it, we've got it. Who needs a Dutch Reformed church? What am I doing here?"

Boy, I asked the questions.

Then, I listened.

And it changed my life.

Chapter 18
Dr. Robert Schuller

Why I preach the way I do

(And yes, I firmly believe in preaching Jesus to the world's lost!)

I asked the Lord just what I was doing, trying to start a church in a Southern California community filled with good churches.

Then, I got quiet and listened for the Lord's answer.

The message I got was:

"The churches in this town are all talking to Christians.

"That's their role. That's what they're supposed to be doing. But I want you to be a pure mission for me. Talk to the 50 percent of the people in town who turn the church off and who don't believe the Bible is the Word of God, who are lost in their sin and shame."

I was to be a missionary — in America!

That created a unique problem for me because in all of my days in theological seminary and in my undergraduate days in Hope College, in all of my Christian teaching, nobody ever taught me how to communicate to sincere, good, beautiful, people who didn't happen to be Christians.

So, I pushed 3,500 doorbells and asked the question, "Are

you an active member of a local church?" If they said, "Yes," I just said, "Good. God bless you. Good-bye." If they said, "No, we don't belong to any church," I said, "Oh, thank God. I'm glad I found you."

When they asked, "Why?" I said, "I'm a minister and I have to learn something. I have to learn why good, beautiful, successful, intelligent, smart people like you do not go to church."

I listened. And listened. About that same time, I took my trip to our world overseas missions and saw that in our missions, we had not only Bible translators and evangelists, but in Africa, we had Hereford cattle, we had chickens, we imported seed, we had agricultural missionaries, we had doctors, we had nurses, we had translators — a whole team — ministering to the whole of the suffering, hurting person.

I came back thinking, "That's what we need. I have to be a missionary to pagan, secular Americans. The way I've got to be a missionary is to minister to their deepest needs. What do they need? They don't need an agricultural missionary. They don't need educational missionaries. They don't need doctors. They don't need nurses." I began ringing doorbells and asking the question, "Is there anything I can do for you?" They would say, "Well, yes. Maybe there is. I have a young person — do you have anything for young people? I'm having problems with my teenager."

I would say, "No, not yet. But someday we will."

I would run across somebody and he would say, "I don't go to church, but frankly, I'm divorced and I'm very lonely. Do you have anything for people like me?"

"No, not yet. But someday we will."

Then I heard, "We're having marriage problems, do you have a marriage counselor?"

"No, not yet, but someday we will."

And that's the way it went.

At the end of my first year, which was 28 years ago, I wrote down the needs of the unchurched persons in that community. I also wrote down their hangups, because I had heard them say, "We don't want to go to church because all these denominations are fighting each other. Everyone thinks he's better than anyone else." Or "All the churches are mixed up in politics. That's all they're preaching — politics." I found out the people had hangups, so I developed a principle. The principle was this: I was convinced that we could grow a church, we could have an effective successful mission for Jesus if I was willing to put the hurts and the needs of the non-Christians above the needs of the Christians. That was it.

Fortunately, it was easy for me to do, because on our opening Sunday, after all the advertising and the doorbell ringing, I had about 50 cars. Now, earlier I'd gone to a Reform Church in Paramount and I'd said, "Can you loan me your choir on Sunday?" They said, "Yes." I said, "How many members in your choir?" They said, "Thirty." "Would you mind all coming in separate cars?" Thus I was assured of 30 cars to begin with. So, we had about 50 cars.

My critic came to me the next morning and said, "Well, you went through with it, didn't you?"

"Yes."

"In that fashion?"

"Yes."

"How many did you have?"

"Fifty cars. I figured about 100 people."

He said, "Is that all?"

I answered, "That's 100 more than last week."

Well, I tell you, it really threw a curve at me. I calculated ... as I came to that church ... I intuitively felt that, aside from the choir that was sitting up there, the people present weren't Christians at all. I was going to use as the opening hymn, "Holy, Holy, Holy." I had to rewrite those words. "Cherubim and Seraphim" — I'd really lose them on that. Right? I've been rewriting the Bible ever since. That's not sacriligious. No. I mean some of these words don't make sense. You have to pick words that communicate the truth but are understandable to people who are totally biblically illiterate.

I'll never forget that I rang one doorbell and found a lovely young lady on the other side of the door. I asked, "Are you an active member of a local church?"

She said, "No."

I said, "Why don't attractive, intelligent people like you go to church? I'm curious." She answered, "Well, my father was Jewish, my mother was Catholic. They decided that I could pick out my own religion when I grew up. In high school I wasn't interested. In college I was busy. When I graduated from college, I got married. That was two years ago and now I've got a little kid and I'm interested in religion for the first time in my life. Tell me. What is your religion like?"

Well, I thought I'd try to build the relationship on the Jewish connection so I said, "As you know, it says in the Old Testament ...." She interrupted me. "What do you mean, the Old Testament?" I answered, "Well, as you know — the Bible is made up of the Old Testament and the New Testament." She said, "Are you telling me you believe in two Bibles?"

True story! Up until that time, a typical Schuller sermon had no less than 50 Bible verses in it, quoted, documented. You wouldn't believe it if you've listened to me on T.V. , but it was true up until then! That blew it all! Because she came to church the following Sunday and she sat there. If she didn't know the difference between the Old Testament and the New Testament,

I couldn't even refer to Abraham. She'd think I was talking about her dad's cousin. True! I couldn't mention the four Gospels. I couldn't say "Ten Commandments."

I had to preach the Word of God without creating roadblocks so her attention span wouldn't be interrupted by wondering, "What does that mean?" and "Who was John?" and "Who was Paul?" and "How does Timothy fit in the whole act?" and "Who in the world are the Corinthians?"

I just couldn't do that. I had to clean it up. Preach Christ! Preach Christ! Preach Christ! That was the message I got. I said, "Lord, how do I preach?"

The answer I continued to get was: "Preach Christ. Preach Christ."

That's how the church started. I did finish after one year what I concluded to be an effective mission to meet the needs of the nonchurched persons in this community. "Wow!" I said. "We're going to need counseling. We're going to need this and this and this." In fact, I calculated it would take nine missionaries with nine separate specialties. And I didn't know what kinds of buildings it would require to carry out the kinds of programs that would meet the needs of the nonchurched people in the community if I wanted to operate as a true foreignmission operation.

When I looked at that, that was impossible. Then I calculated it would take 6,000 members to sustain that kind of a mission. I wrote to my mission board in New York City and said, "I want to remind you that I'm in California. I'm opening a foreign mission station here, and I'd like to qualify for foreign missionary funds."

They said, "Sorry. The land touches the land that touches our board offices, and therefore you don't qualify as a mission station. Now, if you were in the Hawaiian Islands, where there's just water in between, you'd qualify." So I didn't qualify.

This gave me no choice but to pray. I concluded that if it took 6,000 members ... my goodness! 6,000 members, and I had two. Again I prayed. An amazing thing happened. I was 28 years old at the time and I calculated ... well, I hope to work to the age of 68, that's 40 years. Don't say

6,000 members is impossible! I divided 6,000 members by 40 years, and I came up with 150. All I would have to win was 150 members a year. When I retired at the age of 68, we'd have a church of 6,000 members. Not too bad. Right? One hundred and fifty a year, that's only one family a week, because the average family is three members. Father, mother, and throw in a child.

I thought: My goodness, if I can't win one family to Christ a week, then I'm either a lousy product or I'm a miserable communicator and I refused to accept either of those premises. So I made a commitment that, God helping me, we would have a goal of 6,000 members, not because we wanted 6,000 members, but because we needed a financial base for the kind of a mission that would meet the needs of the secular, pagan, cultured Americans.

I did not know what I know now, and that is — Alfred North Whitehead had said it — "Great dreams of great dreamers are never fulfilled, they are always transcended." That is true. We hit our 6,000 membership peak at 15 years instead of 40. That was also when we faced our greatest problem, because, after 15 years, which was 14 years ago, our church building, which was built to seat 1,500 persons so that we could accomodate 3,000 worshipers in two services, which means you service a membership of 6,000, was too small. (In the average church, 50 percent of the membership is the average attendance.) People were sitting outdoors. We knew we needed a larger building.

That was the beginning of a real period of struggle in my life. A real struggle. One company suggested that we let them knock out a wall, and enlarge the building. The engineers said it could be done, but it would cost $2 million and the building would look like a tacky add-on.

The congregation spent $20,000 to study it, hired a professional fund-raiser, and nobody gave anything.

Nobody liked the idea.

It failed, so we wasted two years.

Yet the problem didn't go away. We hired another architect, spent $50,000 and three years. We had some more fund-raising campaigns.

Nobody gave any money.

It was terrible. I mean, we said we needed another building to seat 4,000, 3,000 minimum, and we wanted it to be built as inexpensively as possible. By the time they looked at the buiding codes for the state of California, they found that to build a building for 3,000 people that would be halfway decent, even without a basement, was going to cost us $4 million. And it would be just a great big, black box that didn't glorify God or anyone else.

Nobody gave anything, so by now we'd wasted five years, and people were sitting outdoors, and the problem didn't go away.

Again I prayed for guidance, and into my hands came an invitation to preach in Fort Worth, Texas. That's where I saw Philip Johnson's water gardens. There I decided to go to New York and talk to Philip Johnson. When I met him I said, "Mr. Johnson, we need a larger building to seat 3,000 people. Can you design one for me?"

He said, "Of course."

"I have only one request."

"What's that?"

"I want to make it out of glass, all of it."

Chapter 19

Dr. Robert Schuller

The miracle of the Crystal Cathedral

(How I came to preach in a glass house)

I told Phillip Johnson what I wanted: a church made of glass.

"What? Why?" asked the famous architect.

"Because for six years ... for six years, Mr. Johnson, from 1955 to 1961, I preached under the open sky every Sunday summer, winter, spring and fall, and any pastor who has preached out-of-doors every Sunday for six years is never going to be happy with a plaster roof over his head again. You fall in love with the clouds and the sky and the birds and the trees, and the sunshine and the stars and the moon — and you know what the Bible says: "The heavens declare the glory of God." And you know, then, why God, when He created a place of worship, put it in the garden of Eden. I want to see God's nature all around us."

Philip Johnson said, "All glass?"

"Yes."

"That's impossible!"

I replied, "Mr. Johnson ..." and I pulled out my pocket dictionary. "Read Webster's definition of that word 'impossible.' "

He fingered until he got to the page and then he read it and blushed ... his neck, all the way to the back of his bald head. I mean he got red as a beet.

"Someone with scissors cut the word out," he said. "Well, I'll tell you ... what, how much money can you afford to spend?"

"I'll tell you the honest-to-God truth. Our church has a debt of $3 million. We're amortizing it over 20 years and we're paying it off on schedule. On top of that we borrowed $200,000 on a 24- month note from the Bank of America, just to pay that loan off. That means — we can't afford anything beyond that. So, if you come up with a design that costs $1 million, we can't afford it. If it costs $2 million, we can't afford it. If it costs $4 million, we can't afford it. Consequently, sir, since we can't afford anything, it doesn't make any difference what it costs. It is totally irrelevant. It's going to require a miracle to get $1 million, and I think if it's going to be a miracle for $1 million, as far as God's concerned, $2 million, $3 million, $4 million — what's the difference?"

It was easy to say that then, but a few months later he delivered a little model of the Crystal Cathedral. I'd learned something by this time: no person has a money problem, no church has a money problem, no institution has a money problem, no family has a money problem. I'm not trying to be cute or clever or tricky. It's never a money problem it's always an idea problem. It's really true. There are gobs of money in this world — so much money we can't even comprehend it. If you've got a problem, it means you don't have the share that you want. That's all. So the trick is: how do you get a part of what you need? I happen to believe that God owns the cattle on a thousand hills. That's Scripture, right? So, money flows to the ideas that are God-inspired. I truly believe that. So, when Mr. Johnson delivered a little glass model of the Crystal Cathedral, I took a look at it and said, "That's it." And then I asked him the painful question, "What will it cost?"

"$7 million."

I collapsed. Not quite, but I went into a depression. $7 million! My goodness! We still didn't know how we were going to pay the $200,000 bank loan and the $3 million mortgage on the building. Now $7 million?

I was so depressed, I did something I rarely do in my life. When I do it, I hate to admit it in public, but I've told others, so it's no secret. I did something, and you know that when I do this, I'm in the pits.

I read my own books. Boy, I'm hard up when I read my own books, I can tell you.

I came to that one little chapter — actually, it's a chapter in the current book, Tough Times Never Last, But Tough People Do and it said, "If it's impossible, you pray. You go into two-way prayer. You write down one to ten and you ask God to show you ten ways to do what you already know is impossible."

So I wrote down one to ten just the way I did when the Lord opened up the drive-in theater idea to me in Albuquerque, New Mexico. And I figured — does it still work now, 26 years later? I wrote down one to ten: "How to get $7 million." Number one — the first idea that came into my mind — was a brilliant idea. Get one guy to give $7 million. The second idea that came was: Get seven people to give $1 million each. I can't remember the third. The fourth idea was: I remembered the little country church where I learned to know Jesus; they had three windows on that side, and three windows on the other side and there was a brass plaque under each window as a memorial to someone who'd died in the First World War. I thought, Well, maybe I can sell windows. I've got windows!

So I asked Phil. "How many windows in this place?"

"Ten thousand, six hundred and eighty-six."

Oh, did I have windows! So we sold the windows at $500 a window. $500 a window! $500 times 10,000, that's $5 million. Right? I'll bet there's somebody reading this book who bought a window. I wouldn't be surprised. We sold 10,000 windows in six month's time.

Nobody has a money problem. It's always an idea problem. Ask God for the ideas. It's that simple! Well, the church got built and we made a commitment that we were going to dedicate it debt-free, and that's when I started going through very difficult years because we had been told we needed a basement under it, and that increased the cost from $7 million to $10 million. Then we went into this period — you may not remember it — but there were three years when building materials and labor went up at an inflationary rate just under 30 percent. That's not the average inflation rate but in building materials and labor it went up that much in those three years' time.

Now, if you have a $10 million building project and you add inflation, in one year it's going to increase from $10 million to $13 million. The second year it will jump to $16 million and if it goes on for three years, as it did with us, you're up to $19 million. The cost went from $10 million to $19 million, simply through inflation. When I saw that happening, I called the first donor and said, "I think maybe we want to abort the project."

He said, "Look. I gave you the first $1 million." And he did! That was through two-way prayer, too. I went to a total stranger — never met him before in my life, prayed for guidance and showed him the plan of the Crystal Cathedral and said, "I think I'd like to build it." He declared, "It's great! I think it ought to be built."

I said, "It'll never get built because nobody believes it. But if I had a lead-off gift of $1 million, people would take me seriously." He agreed, "I guess they would." I said, "I'm glad you agree with me. Would you like to have the honor of making that lead-off gift of $1 million?"

Suddenly, he lost all his enthusiasm. He said, "I'd like to, but I can't."

I shrugged, "Well, I understand. May I pray before I leave?" "Yes."

Then I found myself asking questions: "Dear Lord, was it Your idea or my idea that I ask him for $1 million?" I waited. I wasn't manipulating. This was a most sincere, spiritual prayer, I can assure you. The second question was, "Lord, I think You heard that he said he'd like to give $1 million. Is it possible for You to figure out a way for him to do what he'd like to do, but can't?"

The next moring he called me and said, "The building's got to get built. I'll give you a million." Within 60 days, we had stock in his company: it was converted, after commission, to $987,000 cash in the savings account. How does that grab you? Incredible! It was a miracle as far as I was concerned.

When it looked as though the cost was going up to $19 million, I stated: "I think I'll give you your money back.

He protested, "Oh, no you won't. I gave the money for the Cathedral, and you don't have the money to build it. I don't care if it costs $30 million or $40 million, at least DIG A HOLE!"

I argued, "I don't want to dig a hole and just sit there with a hole in the ground! What am I going to do with a hole? You can't sell it. I mean — how can you get a hold of it? Try to put it in a truck and the truck would fall in before you got it in the truck." So I had a lot of fun with that one. But he kept insisting, "Dig a hole."

So I finally said, "OK."

We went to the contractor who told us, "I'll tell you what I can do. For $9 million, I can build a shell. The doors will be boarded up — it will be just a shell — but at least the windows will be in." That was important. I had to deliver, you know, because by this time we'd spent a lot of front money. Then he said, "I'll tell you what we'll do. We'll dig the hole, then after three months, I'll need this much and after four months, I'll need that much, and so we'll keep going. You put in the money and if the money comes — fine! If not, we stop."

Wow!

I can't tell the whole story in the space allotted here, but I'll tell you one thing — we came to a screeching halt again because we didn't have any more money. That was on September 15, actually — because we had to put in $1.5 million and there was no way we could find it. I had sold everything I owned to deliver a cash gift of 150,000, which was the sum total of my net worth at that time. Gave it all in one offering in the church for a million-dollar offering. I had nothing left to give. I had exhausted all possibilities.

You know I have a page in the book, *Tough Times Never Last, But Tough People Do*, and that page is: "When you've exhausted all possibilities, remember this — you haven't.

It's really true, because you can still pray. You can still pray! That's exactly what I did. It was the middle of August and I got a letter, and I needed $1.5 million by September or construction would stop. First of all, I got a letter from Ray Kroc of McDonald's Hamburgers. I'd never met the guy. He saw a picture of the building and said it was great and it ought to be built and he enclosed a check in six figures. I got another check for $150,000 — unsolicited — from another corporate chief in Michigan. Unsolicited! That's $250,000 out of the blue. That's still $1 million short, but it was encouraging.

During that same week's time, I got a letter from a man in Chicago, saying, "I flipped your program on last Sunday and I saw a picture of this cathedral you're building. That's fantastic! What is the financial status of the project? Is it all underwritten or would another $1 million gift from an old man in Chicago be helpful?" I couldn't believe it.

The first thing I did was check the guy out to see that he wasn't a flake. I had so many offers of $1 million, and $10 million gifts and gold mines, and you name it. But, we checked the guy out and found that he was the founder and chairman of a corporation that had done $1.5 billion in sales the previous year, and ranked in the top 50 in the Fortune 400 companies. That's not exactly a flaky character.

I remember he said in a letter, "You don't have to come and see me about this. We can handle it all by letter. You don't have to call."

I decided to call. I called at his home. By now it was the tenth of September. I met one of the most beautiful Christians I've ever met in my life. I said, "You know, the truth is, we need another $1.2 million by the fifteenth. That's next week. Or construction stops."

He looked at his wife and said, "Mary, I don't think that date will be a problem, do you?" And she said, "No." He told me, "You just go home and keep preaching those good sermons, Reverend. I just love those sermons. You'll have your check."

Sure enough, four days later, I got a check from him, a cashier's check, for $1 million. I deposited that check in the bank myself.

Then we had a good year in income, and we kept construction going, but we needed another $1 million in February. The old gentleman invited me to his 82nd birthday party. I went. There were seven of us at the country club and he said, "Dr. Schuller, on my birthday, I can be selfish. Right?"

"Right."

He said, "Right. I'm going to do something that I get a big kick out of doing. It might embarrass you if I told you, so I put it in this letter and you can read it on the way to the airport."

I got in the car and opened the envelope. Inside there was a note. He wrote: "I've discovered that I get my best kicks by giving people big surprises. I have a feeling you could use another gift." And enclosed was another check for $1 million. Unsolicited! Unsolicited!

Finally, by the time we turned the key, the building cost us $20 million — but it was debt free!

I've learned in my simple witness that you choose the dream. From that point on, the dream will shape your future. So begin by prayer — two-way prayer — and ask God what He wants you to do and make your thinking big enough for God to fit in!

Remember this: You choose the size of your dream and from that point on the dream will decide how far you go and how big you become for God and His glory.

The second lesson I've learned is that you have to plan in the Spirit, because if you fail to plan, you are planning to fail.

Plan to succeed and you'll succeed with your plan.

The next thing I've learned is: inch by inch, anything's a cinch! What we have today happened because we had a 40-year plan. We've used up 29 years at this point. We have 11 years to go.

But inch by inch, anything's a cinch. The third thing I've learned is: *There is no gain without pain.* More than once — in fact, I can think of 12 times in the past 29 years — I have wanted to quit and walk away from it so badly! There was a time when I thought I couldn't handle it anymore. That's when I had my greatest miracle with Jesus who reached down with an invisible finger into my brain in the middle of a night and took away my anxiety and gave me a miracle of healing.

But there is no gain without pain. You fail to plan and you're planning to fail. Then I've learned that the secret of success is to find a need and fill it.

Finally, I've learned that it's impossible to succeed unless you constantly are in the servant role, which means — "God, what do You want me to do?" All this requires one simple thing:

Obedience.

Obedience to the Spirit's leading. It's impossible to succeed then, without doing a lot of good for a lot of people.

As you shape the dreams for your ministry and your church — first, get in tune with God's Spirit. Then, you're going to get an idea that's impossible. So, get in touch with God's people. They can make the impossible, possible. Finally, get in time with God's calendar. He may say, "Move fast!" or He may say, "Slow down."

It took us from the time we began to solve our building problems until the cathedral was opened; it took 12 years. Three architectural plans. Two financial failures. But believe God's promise. He rewards the men and women of faith. Just dare to believe the biggest dream.

A favorite story of mine wraps up what I have said.

A man was fishing. A tourist came along and watched him. He would catch a fish and then measure it with a ruler that was ten inches long. If the fish was eight or nine or seven inches, he would keep it. But some were longer — 11, 12 inches.

He threw them back in.

The tourist said, "What's the big idea? Why do you keep the little fish and throw big ones away?"

"Because," the man said, "my frying pan is only ten inches wide."

Now I'm going to tell you the name of that fisherman. *You're looking at him.* I think you look at that fisherman every morning in the mirror, too. I'll prove it to you.

The biggest idea God ever gave you — you threw away! *Right away!* It scared the daylights out of you, because you knew it was impossible, and you'd fail.

The truth is ... He was setting you up for what could have been the greatest miracle of you life!

A new beginning
(God has an adventure ahead for you!)

I believe in our lifetime we are seeing, by and through the power of the Holy Spirit, the church of the Lord Jesus Christ coming together in a way it never has in the history of the church, at least in our generation.

For a number of years I've had a growing conviction that the very heartthrob of God is going to be manifested in a most remarkable way in our inner cities. It was not my choice to become a pastor in the inner city, as far as my looking for that role in my ministry. But the Lord called me in a most unusual way.

I was in Memphis, Tennessee. We had raised up a church there. It was a wonderful church, wonderful people. My wife and I were exceedingly happy in our ministry. We expected to stay there the rest of our lives. In fact, we had just built a beautiful new home and had only lived in it long enough to get the poison ivy out of the oak trees, get the yard fixed up right and the house comfortable. But in my spirit began to well up — Washington, D.C. I didn't know anything about Washington, except that it was our nation's Capital and as a teenager I had visited it as a tourist. Yet this kept welling up in my heart and spirit. When I talked about it a little bit, my wife was unconcerned. One evening this feeling came to be so great within my spirit that the Lord and I talked about it all night long. Early that next morning I was heading toward my bedroom when I met my wife. She had a smile on her face, we greeted each other and I said, "Honey, we're going to go to Washington."

Well, she'd heard that before, so she paid no real attention. So I said, "Are you ready to go?"

"Oh, yes."

"Good. Let's sell the house." I really got her attention. She turned around and retreated back to the bedroom and locked the door. She stayed in there until afternoon. Then she came out with a smile on her face, her eyes very red, her nose very red and she said, "Honey, I'm ready."

The next Sunday morning, without ever having come here to Washington, not knowing anything about it, I resigned our wonderful church. I immediately left for Washington, not knowing anyone in the Capital. Well, the Lord has given us a wonderful, exciting time here for almost 29 years. It has been glorious and rewarding. The Lord has been very gracious. We've had an exciting time.

But I have come more and more to believe with great conviction that the church is going to find its natural habitat, its natural real place, in the inner cities. When the Apostle Paul left from Antioch, it was not out in the countryside he went — but into metropolitan areas. And I suspect they had problems almost as great in his time as we have in our day. Different, maybe, but as great.

I believe our God has not overlooked the decay we have seen in our inner cities. It's amazing what has happened in the last few years. Who would have ever believed that many of our large metropolitan cities are on the verge of bankruptcy? Twenty years ago we couldn't conceive that such a thing would have happened. And the church in many cases has left the inner city. (Fine. We have a lot of wonderful churches in the suburban areas. That ought to be. It's proper and right.) But God has not overlooked all the problems that are among the poor, the disenfranchised, the helpless and, in many cases, the hopeless. I believe with all my heart, that in the years immediately ahead of us — and it has already begun to happen — there is going to come a focus on the inner cities of our nation and of the world. We are going to see God arise in our inner cities as we have never dreamed or even imagined. I believe that's where the action is going to be in the years immediately ahead of us. I believe that in the 1980s, God is going to move in our inner cities in a measure and in a way that we never dreamed of. It's happening. It's really happening. I believe we're going to see it escalate in a most remarkable way.

In the last few weeks the book of First John has captured my attention. Here are two or three verses that describe the normality of the Christian church, at least from John's perspective and, I believe, from the perspective of the Holy Spirit. They speak about the fellowship we have with God and with one another.

"That which was from the beginning which we have heard, which we have seen with our eyes, which we have looked upon, and our hands have handled, concerning the word of life — the life was manifested, and we have seen it and bear witness, and declare to you that eternal life which was with the Father and was manifested to us, that which we have seen and heard, we declare to you, that you also may have fellowship with us and truly our fellowship is with the Father and with His Son, Jesus Christ. We write this to you — that your joy may be full.

"This is the message that we have heard from him and declare to you: God is light; and in Him is no darkness at all. If we say we have fellowship with Him while we walk in darkness, we lie and do not practice the truth. But if we walk in the light, as He is in the light, we have fellowship one with another, and the blood of Jesus Christ continuously cleanses us from all sin."

The church of the Lord Jesus Christ is beginning to recognize that indeed it is the Body of the Lord Jesus Christ. This is my hope; this is my excitement; this is my expectation. I am seeing it happen. In the past few years, increasingly so. Articles everywhere are written, people are talking about the inner cities and God is moving mightily. I believe that God has allowed the inner city problems to escalate until we have recognized that there is not only a political solution.

Of course, we need every political solution that we can possibly get. Thank God for the concern of the government! But God will not allow these problems that He has let come to pass be solved without the church of the Lord Jesus Christ really becoming involved. And that's the call to the church.

The apostle excites me in the extent that most of his sermons were his testimony. Right at the last he said, "I was not disobedient to the heavenly vision."

When God laid upon my heart to come to Washington, D.C., not knowing anyone, we sold our house, resigned the church and came. I never went back. I sent for my wife, family, associates and a few other workers and we moved to Washington, D.C. The Lord had made it clear to me that we were to be in the city proper.

We started in the old Turner's Arena. We were told it had been a stable for the mounted police horses. It had the smell still, even though it was an arena. It was in one of the roughest areas in D.C. But God was there. I mean God met us.

People off the street ... they just came. And God met us. This was back in 1955. In those days throughout the world the Lord was pouring out His Spirit in a way that I hadn't known before. There were great healing services. The miraculous was happening. God moved mightily in our midst. We had 14 services a week. Every afternoon, every night, three on Sunday. People would leave their work and come. I thought it was wonderful. However, I came to understand it was not enough just to have an evangelistic church and "save souls." It had to be more than just saving souls. I understood then that we must begin to have a teaching church.

The ministry of the church is to equip the saints. It is important not only to save souls. You must save lives. Because maybe, just maybe, you might be able to save a soul without saving a life. It seems to be so. The thief on the cross said to Jesus, "Remember me." And Jesus said, "Today you will be with Me in Paradise." Obviously his soul was saved, but his life was lost.

It is the church's business to save lives. If you really save lives, you can rest assured you'll be saving souls. But there is a possibility I am convinced of: of saving souls and losing lives. The inheritance of Christ is in the saints. It's in the lives of the people He's redeemed here and now. That's His inheritance. He has called us to manifest Himself by and through the power of the Holy Spirit in this life, in these mortal bodies, Christ incarnate. Thank God! It was a glorious day when I became aware of the fact that we have the possibility as members in the Body of Christ in sharing in the Incarnation, which is an ongoing, glorious, wonderful reality in the world today for the church which is His Body.

So we became a teaching church. That was difficult, because when you have a "bless me" church for a long time, it is very difficult to get people interested in settling down and becoming prepared and ready to be a serving church. We had seemingly done right well as a "bless me" church. Thank God for His blessings. How we need His blessings! But then again, if indeed the church is the Body of Christ, we are to be a serving church.

Now, by God's grace, we have come, in some small way, to enter into that ministry which I feel is perhaps one of the most meaningful needs to build a church in the inner city. I was told this last fall: that we register something more than 2,000 adults alone in a nine-month course. We have registered nine-month graded courses, exams, etc. This then gives the meat to what the Apostle Paul had to say in Ephesians, that the work, the ministry is to equip the saints. We are endeavoring to bring that into some kind of meaningful reality.

Along with the teaching church, we have come to understand in our experience that we must also have a worshiping church. I was an eager beaver for the Lord Jesus Christ to save the lost, as most evangelicals are, I suppose. Pentecostals certainly are. In my being caught up in serving the Lord, I was so anxious to do exploits it was a revelation for me to recognize that the first calling of every child of God that is born of the Spirit is the highest ministry that one can be called to. Every born-again believer is called to the highest ministry in the church — to be a worshiper! To worship the Lord.

I was not aware of the fact that I could serve God as a worshiper. That was a revelation. It also became a very real part of our teaching ministry, that we are first called to worship God. It became rather extraordinary in my understanding to see that when Jesus was in the wilderness Satan bargained with Him and said, "Look, You've come after the kingdoms of the world. I have them and they are mine to give to whomsoever I choose. The price is only that You fall down and worship me."

And Jesus said, "It is written, 'Thou shalt worship the Lord thy God and Him only shalt thou serve.' " Worshiping and serving certainly are part of the same. You cannot really worship God unless you are first a servant. But it's possible to be a servant and not to be a worshiper also. These two must be in balance.

So beginning to teach in our church was a very different transition because we had our sanctuary filled with people. It was a joy to come on Sunday morning and see the place packed and jammed, and in some cases, people standing even after extra chairs had been put up. Sunday after Sunday that happened. But when we started teaching and began to try to learn to worship the Lord in spirit and in truth, as we understood the Bible to teach, one by one people we loved, people with whom we had wonderful fellowship, didn't show up as frequently. Finally, we had only about one-third of our sanctuary filled with people. We didn't know what had happened to all those wonderful, good people that we loved so very, very much.

It's a heartbreak for any pastor. In fact it got so bad that we roped off two-thirds of the sanctuary so we could get our people in one little place to feel as though we were together. After having great numbers of people for several years we had only this handful, only about 300 people in place of what we had been accustomed to.

Whereas before we had always had visitors, during those two or three years, I do not believe we had even one. As miraculously as the Lord had blessed us in the years before by sending people in, just as miraculously in the reverse — wow! But we carried on.

In the midst of those two or three years of finding what to us was God's calling in a whole new dimension, He spoke to us prophetically and said, "Arise and build." At that time we had a sanctuary in an old theater we had converted which would seat about 800 people. We crammed 1,000 in it many times.

"Arise and build." Fine! That's great! But, to begin with, in the inner city, where do you find a piece of land to buy? Well, we found a piece of land. It had a big price tag on it. How do we buy it? At that time, there were 250, maybe 300 of us. Most were just dayworkers — no professionals whatsoever. How then were we to rise and build, pray tell? We already had more room than we needed!

Well, we'd learned to worship — to some degree at least. So I told the people what God had spoken and we paid a little money down on a piece of property, drew up some plans for a sanctuary that would seat 2,000 people. Now, that's madness! But God actually spoke that to us. We had a little peice of ground, 27,000 square feet, which is just a mite more than a half acre on which to build. The sanctuary which was to seat 2,000 people with theater seats, turned out to seat only 1,800. We put a few chairs in the aisle occasionally now, so we do get our 2,000 in.

How are we going to build this? No banking institution would look at us! We're in the red-lined area — the inner city — to begin with. There was no way to get a loan. Even if we were in a choice place where loans were considered viable, they would never lend to us. We were just a little church. I went to the congregation and said, "You know, if we can get all the men who have a financial rating, and if they're willing to sign a note collectively, maybe we can borrow some money." All of the men and ladies both were ready to sign anything. But none of them had even a checking account, much less a savings account.

I took those signatures down to the bank. They wrapped them up after looking over them for a week, and sent them all back and said, "Sorry." So what could we do?

Well, the Lord had said, "Arise and build," so we did. I'll never forget the day we went out on that little lot and the handful of us had a groundbreaking service. We had $35,000 in our building fund. The church was its own general contractor, but we had subcontractors. We sought to put to work everybody in our congregation who didn't have a job. We actually taught young men how to read a ruler. Our scheme was that in the building of the church we could teach trades and a lot of our people who didn't have a trade could have jobs. We felt it was of the Lord. Hopefully, we'd put some of our folks in business because of the experience of building our church.

But we had another problem. When it came to building a church this size, steel erection and all that, we didn't have any way to take care of that. So we had to sublet a lot of the contracts — the heating, the cooling, the steelwork and so forth. How were we going to do that?

The subcontractors would come and offer a bid and they would say, "Now, of course, you have this money in escrow?" Why, we didn't have any money in escrow at all, but we weren't going to tell anybody! How do you get around that? We said, "Sure, we'll be glad to give you proper guarantee that you'll be paid when you're finished. But, by the same token, we'd like a performance bond from you." They'd kind of look down a little bit because we knew it was going to cost them something and they'd given us a good bid. Then we'd say, "I'll tell you what. You forego our escrow account and we'll forego your bond." When they signed the contracts the building began to go up.

One of my minister friends came by when the steel structure was all up and some of the floors were poured. A four-story building. I took him through the structure. After we had taken the tour (it took about an hour) we got in the car and drove down the road. He was quiet as could be. He was a traveled man — all over the world — a wonderful man of God. Finally, he broke the silence and said, "I want to ask you a question." He'd been preaching for me over in that other place with only a handful of people.

I said, "Yes, what's that?"

"What on earth are you ever going to do with that building if you ever do finish it?" I'd never been asked that before!

I looked straight at him. I had to be honest with him. I said, "I haven't the slighest idea in the world." And I didn't! But I knew that God had spoken.

Do you know how we paid for that building? The Lord gave me a plan. It wouldn't work again. I've never seen God work a miracle the same way twice. He's a God of variety. Principles, but not in the identical way.

Every Sunday we worshiped the Lord, we rejoiced before Him. Many times there was a prophetic word that was encouraging and uplifting. Then each Sunday I stood up and announced to the people that for this week we needed only so many thousands of dollars to be current. And here was this little handful of people. I said it with faith and with gusto as best I could. When I told the people how much we needed, we raised our hands in praise and thanked the Lord for it. Then we brought in a great big bowl, a gold bowl. Well, really, it was a dough-mixing bowl that we'd painted gold. And we put it on a pedestal right in front. As we began to praise the Lord for meeting the need for that week, the people marched out of the aisles and put their offerings into that bowl. And we paid as we built by a miracle of God.

"But you wouldn't take advantage of people like that, would you, pastor? Take their money away from them?" You might ask me.

I would like you to come and talk with our people. I would like you to ask them what God did for them. I have never heard such exciting testimonies.

Let me tell you about one. She was from Jamaica. And she was a domestic. She came to me, and in her Jamaican accent said, "Pastor, I've been tryin' to get $1,000 together." She'd never seen $1,000 in her life. "Other people are bringin' in

their money." While we were building, there were people —
many, many people who had never seen $1,000 in their lives
— who went out to borrow money. Many of them succeeded
in borrowing $1,000 to give.

They wouldn't wait until Sunday. They would come at ten
or eleven at night, knocking on my door, and say, "Pastor, I
got it! I got it! I got it!" They were so happy they didn't know
what to do. And this little lady said, "Pastor, everybody else
is giving and I can't give."

I said, "Go down to such and such a bank." I knew one of
the officers down there. "Go see him and tell him to let you
have $1,000."

A day or two later this bank officer called me up and said,
"Look, pastor, there's this lady down here. There's no way!
If I give her $1,000, she'll never be able to pay it back on her
income. Not only that. If she would by some miracle pay it
back, she'd want to come back and borrow another $1,000.
It's just not good business."

I said, "Please, sir, give her the money." The next Sunday
this dear lady came rejoicing. She had her $1,000. Rather than
taking a year to pay it back, she paid it back in six months.
Then, just as the banker said, she borrowed another $1,000.
She paid that back in six months. And then, just as the banker
said, she borrowed another $1,000. She paid that back in six
months. About that time we had the building finished. She
went back to the banker and borrowed another $1,000 to take
a vacation back home in Jamaica. And she paid that back. She's
got credit!

Many stories I could tell you about how
God met us in such a miraculous way. Those were great, wonderful days.

When we moved into this monstrosity of a building — to
us it was — it was the most humbling thing that I have ever
experienced in my life. Platform so high, 250 to 300 people

sitting in the two or three rows right in front of us, and here I am, a half mile away, standing up there looking down. Try as we might, nobody would come see us.

We had paid all our bills except ... you're supposed to hold back five or ten percent on a subcontract, so we'd withheld that but paid everything else. When the person who had given us the largest bid, which was for the steel construction, had finished his part of the job, I went down to the bank with him and we paid him off in full. I told him how we started.

When he heard that we had had no money, yet had signed that big contract with him, although I had paid him off and he had the check in his hands, I thought he was going to faint.

We had these ten percents or five percents on heating and a few of the other contracts. When we stuck a lot of those together, it totaled up to around $100,000. We were all working together. At night the whole congregation came out and chipped cement and rolled things around and moved concrete blocks. We learned what it was to have community, to be together with great joy and gusto. But this great amount hung over our heads.

Everybody came in and sat down and said, "Hallelujah! We made it!" The creditors started coming. It was a real crunch as far as the building market was concerned.

But we learned how to use the name of Jesus. I was so intimidated. I felt so badly. It was the first time in my life I had ever been behind in our debts. I mean really behind — more than 60 days. In the building business 60 days is somewhat current.

Now we'd gotten behind on just that last little bit. It was so burdening my spirit I called my elders in. I told them the story. I was crying; I needed some sympathy. My credibility was gone. We'd always paid our debts.

One of my elders — a black man — looked at me. A little

grin came across his face. He said, "Pastor, now you know what it is like." That's all the sympathy I got and that's what I needed. I shaped up, squared my shoulders and prayed.

We have learned that if we truly worship, we must be a loving, caring church. That's what we're about now: to learn to serve the Lord as we serve the Body of the Lord Jesus Christ. In serving the Body of the Lord Jesus Christ, loving and serving one another, we are learning a little more about what it is to be true worshipers of the Lord Jesus Christ. We're on a journey. It's exciting. We don't know exactly where the end is going to be, except now there are many churches coming together and joining hands. We believe that Washington, D.C., is a city set on a hill. We see that in our spirits. We see it in our hearts. We see it by faith. It is a city set on a hill to be a light for the Lord Jesus Christ who is Lord of lords and King of kings. We're thrilled to be in that great, wonderful army.

These are great days in which we live! I hope and trust that you now have a whole new expectancy of God moving mightily in the inner cities all over this nation and over the world.

Chapter 21

Dr. Samuel Hines

Faith brings reconciliation

(That means holding no more grudges!)

From where I sit, I look at the Scriptures, at history, at the whole body of recorded and developing revelation and I discern that God has a one-item agenda — reconciliation!

Ever since sin interrupted the order and blessing of God's creation, that item has not changed. It is still reconciliation! I see the church as having no option but to witness to the reconciling work of God in His Son. By His sacrifice the way is cleared for all men to be completely changed! By the way — that's what the word reconcile means.

It's not just a few fellows back-slapping each other and having a few nice social chit-chats and making a few social adjustments to each other culturally. The biblical word for reconcile means "to completely change." And that change, the Scriptures maintain, is necessary if sinners are ever to be related to God and one another.

What reconciliation does is to set the world right. It is the only way the fallen, sinful world can be set right. If millions of people join our churches without reconciliation, we will have big churches, but the world will not be set right.

Reconciliation is God's plan to change the picture completely for the whole creation and to make every sinner savable — that's reconciliation. Reconciliation is God's way of revealing and releasing new vital possibilities for all of us in our struggles and in our frustration.

Reconciliation reverses the effect of sin objectively. That's from God's perspective. It reverses the effect of sin in the human race and announces to the whole world, to every creature, that mankind can now — not in some distant milennium — be restored to God's original plan of unity and beauty. That's reconciliation!

God made a great and beautiful and glorious world and looked upon it and said, "Ah! That's good!" Then He made man and said, "That's very good!" Next He said , "It's not good that man should be alone." Because man alone would become an egotist wrapped up in himself and become a diminishing person, God established community. That's what men and women are all about — not the sexual rot that we have in the world today.

Men and women are about community — God's original plan for this universe. The result of sin is the upset and drastic cancellation of the arrangement that God has made. Reconciliation is God's provision to restore His plan to the world. Reconciliation removes the inevitable curse of death which sin deserves — for the wages of sin is death.

Jesus took upon Himself what we had coming to us and now, since He died for us, we can abide with Him. We can live with the resurrected Christ forever more. Sin cannot catch up with us for, in Christ, we are covered. That's reconciliation!

When I use the word "reconciliation," I always have to define it, for other people are always anxious to define it for me and weaken its meaning. Some years ago I was in South Africa preaching reconciliation when a very brilliant, astute theologian (of radical persuasion) pointed his accusing finger across the table to me and said, "Sam Hines, you're 10 years — 20 years — maybe 50 years too late. There is no time for reconciliation. We need revolution." (By the way — he wasn't black, either — in case you think he was).

He said, "We need revolution in South Africa to lift the burden off the people's backs. Reconciliation is too soft. We need revolution."

By that time he had touched my red button! Forgetting where I was and who I was supposed to be, I jumped up in that prestigious hall and said, "Sir! I will not allow you to define my terms and then judge me by your definition. Let me define my own terms for you — then you make your own judgment." I said further, "Reconciliation is not weak and namby-pamby and watery as you suggest. Reconciliation is bloody. Here is the difference. The revolutionary says, "The world is in bad shape and needs to be changed — must be changed and if anybody gets in my way — if anybody interrupts me — I'll kill him!"

Reconciliation is the most explosive and expensive undertaking in the world. It is the basis of world change. Without it you and I have no hope! No church program, no government programs, no social programs, no private programs, no public programs, no legislation, no caucuses will be able to change the world unless there is reconciliation. Your job and mine is to preach it, practice it, promote it, proclaim it, advertise it and make it visible to those around us. It ain't easy!

Reconciliation. The whole book of Ephesians, which I hope you read and study and memorize and dream about — I hope you soak it up — for one message, which is, that God has one agenda in the world. His agenda is to bring all things together in Christ Jesus. God has a transcending, superior program to create this Christ-centered universe. Talk about high tech! That's God's agenda.

I came upon a little verse that took on new meaning for

me when I began to learn Greek in my studies. II Corinthians 5:14 says, "The love of Christ constraineth us." I'd heard all this preaching about the love of Christ impelling us, the love of Christ compelling us, the love of Christ dwelling in us, the love of Christ driving us, but suddenly in that Greek class, I came upon a new word for compel, for drive, synŏchi. It means "to hold together." The love of Christ holds us together. Did you get that? It holds us together as a reconcilable community before Him — completely changed. In the change, it has developed a new cohesiveness. It does stick!

I don't know how you understand that, but I tell you that if church growth doesn't include that, I have no use for it. Church growth is not the aggregate of individuals, it's not pearls or beads on a string — each separate, prosperous, blessed, sanctified, satisfied, petrified and all the rest of it. A nice crowd of saved people sitting in comfortable pews will not change this world if that's all that happens. They must stick together. Something must make them cohesive, make them hold fast.

Consider the words, *"The love of Christ constraineth us because we are thus judged, that if one died for all, then they are all dead, but He died for all so that they that live should* live *not ~~die~~ for themselves, but unto Him which died and rose again."* Do you get the all-ness about this passage?

Reconciliation is not a few peoples' fad. It is not just Hines' hobbyhorse. Reconciliation is the primary agenda of the body of Christ. What this text says is that God has a real way of bringing us together. Jew or Gentile, bond or free, educated or uneducated, whether in Africa of Asia or Europe or America or the islands of the sea, black or white, rich or poor, high or low, religious or irreligious, infidel or heathen, whatever we are — God just throws all of us together. You know what God says? "All have sinned" — the whole bunch of us!

You know what more He says? I have reconciled all of you! The whole bunch of you! That brought a brand-new thing to my ministry. I no longer go out trying to reconcile and pressure and force people to work out some plan of reconciliation. My job is to go out in the world announcing that God has reconciled!

If I understand my Bible right, He has reconciled everybody — the born and unborn. As one of you, I am against abortion because those who would be aborted are among those whom God has reconciled. He has reconciled everybody objectively. He has reconciled everyone objectively on the same basis. Whether you are a millionaire or a pauper, you are reconciled with God on the same basis.

If you know the Bible from cover to cover or if you've never heard a word of Scripture — you are on the same basis. If you belong to every church in town or if you don't belong to any — you have been reconciled on the same basis. The only trouble is — some have accepted it, some have not.

My job is to go out and announce it to everybody and just rejoice upon seeing people accept it and experience the complete change that was accomplished two thousand years ago.

The Scripture also says, *"Wherefore henceforth know we no man after the flesh."* Did you get that? *"Though we know no man after the flesh, yet now and henceforth know we no more. Therefore if any man be in Christ Jesus, he is a new creature. Old things pass away, old things become new and all things become new and all things are of God who has reconciled us to Himself by Jesus Christ who has given us the ministry of reconciliation."*

If you are reconciled and you understand reconciliation, you get beyond all the normal barriers — nationalism (I didn't say there was anything wrong with nationhood), racism (nothing wrong with race), culture, limitations, assumptions — if you are living in any of these, then you are living as the unreconciled — still living unto yourself. You are reconciled if you no longer live by other people's expectation, you no longer live according to your temptation, your frustrations, because you're held together by Christ's love — the love that made Him die for sinners, that love that brought Him from the tomb, the love that brought Him back to life so that you and I might live with Him; so that those of us who are so held together live in spite of our environment — an environment that tends to pull us apart in parties and politics and into material compartments of life and academic divisions of social structures and a society that's determined to tear us up into bits and pieces and to tell me that I'm better than you and to tell you that you're better than I. Society is determined to make us enemies, and not friends — to alienate us and pulverize us and make us look suspiciously and hatefully at each other. But reconciled people stick together!

Pick up the divine perspective: Know no man after the flesh because reconciled people have moved, they have relocated and that's what is going to bring us together — when we all find our relocation! Then we no longer will be living in the suburbs of the inner city; we no longer will be living in wealth and in squallor; we no longer will be living as the haves and haves-nots; we will all be living in Christ Jesus — that's relocation.

"Old things pass away and all things become new." That's the word that we always keep omitting, the word "all." I pastor a predominantly black church and have to constantly remind my church that the world is not black. I hope you whites remind your churches that the world is not white. I remind mine that all of us are reconciled — not on the basis of race, but the basis of grace, and that grace is not in a culture or a system, but in a person that is Jesus Christ.

You will notice that the Bible never says that God is "reconciled." It never says it, because that would be wrong.

It is blasphemous to say that. We are reconciled to God — because reconciled means "to completely change." How are you going to completely change God and still have God? No, He doesn't have to change to our whims and fancies; He doesn't change to adjust to our cultural and situational pattern. We change and since we can't do it all by ourselves, He does it for us in Jesus Christ.

Reconciliation is so precious to my heart because I'm from Jamaica, born in a little town called Salona del Mar — a Spanish name showing the Spanish were there. And the Spaniards did not come to Jamaica to reconcile. The came in 1498 to get rich and they killed off all the Indians — so you don't have any of the original population in Jamaica — not one. All dead! Those who weren't killed purposely just died from the diseases brought by the Spaniards.

The English came in 1655. For 300 years they ruled Jamaica and taught me to sing, *Rule Britannia* — "Britannia rules the waves; Britannia never, never slaves." And I sang that lustily in my colonial ignorance.

In a way, the Lord saved me on that little island. One day my heart ached. Somebody had lied about me and I wanted to smack her so badly. My father was the pastor of the church and the lady organist told a lie. My father whipped me and I was ready to have a revolution. That Sunday evening, with bitterness in my heart, waiting for that service to be dismissed so that I could carry out some plot of vengeance, the Lord spoke.

I responded that I wasn't going to that funny altar where they sang those funny hymns. I told my head I wasn't going, I told my feet I wasn't going, and I told my heart I wasn't going — I must have missed something because I went anyway!

I found the Lord! And guess what He did? Not the second, third, fourth thing He did, but the first thing was to give me love for that liar. Oh, I know she lied about me, but He gave me a love for her that wouldn't quit. She's never apologized to me to this day, but I believe she must have talked to the Lord about it — for I think she's going to heaven. I hope to see her in heaven and I'm going to love her there, too.

I suddenly discovered that I was no better than she. I couldn't judge her because she and I have come to the same reconciliation to come to God. And ever since that time, God has put it in my heart to love people — all people — particularly those who hurt me and those who really give me a hard time. I should just love them because I have no right to do anything else.

When I got to Washington, D.C., 15 years ago, I asked: "Lord, why am I here?" A bit late to ask, but anyway I did. "Why did I leave the magnificent climate of tropical Jamaica with its sunshine and its beaches to come to Washington? My friend, Howard Lockingay, was in Jamaica as a speaker the year I was leaving and he said, "Sam, I hear you are going to America. What for?"

I said, "To preach, to pastor.

He said, "Where?"

"In Washington, D.C."

"Why?"

"Why? Because the Lord has called me to go there."

About two or three years after I came to Washington, I appreciated his statement, but I thank God that He brought me here. The Lord told me when He brought me that I was here for one purpose. He told me in plain, good English.

Reconciliation. He told me once, twice — I don't know how many times. Every time I tried to get around it, He said it again.

And so I took the book of Ephesians and almost saturated my people with it. I preached it for nearly eighteen months

— "Ephesians, Ephesians, Ephesians. Reconciliation, reconciliation, reconciliation." I took them on retreats until they wondered what happened.

"Reconciliation, reconciliation, reconciliation," — the more I taught it, the less I saw of it. I kept preaching it, doing it, sharing it and I got them to work up a statement which I can't remember now myself. When I get excited, I forget it.

Here it is: "*We are ambassadors for Christ in the nation's capital, committed to be a totally open, evangelistic, metropolitan, caring fellowship of believers. To this end we are being disciplined in a community of Christian faith, centered in the love of Jesus Christ, administered by the Holy Spirit. We have covenanted to honor God, obey His Word, celebrate His grace, demonstrate a life-style of servanthood, and accordingly, we seek to proclaim to the whole world a full-cycle ministry of reconciliation.*" I want you to know that big statement took three and a half years to work out!

Then we began to ask, "How do we practice this?" When we were trying to find how to practice it, God sent me a man by the name of John Staggers — "Mr. Reconciliation" himself — a man whom God has put into his heart the whole world. Loves everybody! God sent him into my life as a brother and in the church as a leader in the community and as a pacesetter and an agent of change.

John has given his life over the years to bringing people together in Christ. He used to do it by just bringing people together, but then he met Christ and through John and John's team, we worked out the whole ministry of reconciliation — the powerful, the powerless, the rich, the poor, Armenians, Calvinists, non-Pentecostals and Charismatics. The whole bunch has just recognized that what doctrine and dogma could not do for you, a mission will do. Mission has brought us together in Washington.

I don't wear any labels. If you call me a liberal, I'm very hurt. If you call me a conservative, I'm equally hurt. I'm just

a biblical Christian. Keep your labels — wear them if you want
to — but don't pin them on me!

We're trying to serve the whole man. We treat street people like those whom God has reconciled;. We treat alcoholics
like those whom God has reconciled. We treat unwed mothers
like those whom God has reconciled. We treat some people
who have been involved in abortion like those whom God
has reconciled. I try to announce to them that they have a
heritage that they know nothing about — that they have been
reconciled in Christ.

The National Presbyterian Church is a nice, prestigious,
wealthy, affluent, uptown church that joined with our little
church. Our two churches got together. One preacher is tall
and lanky and white and Calvinist and the other is short and
black and fat and Wesleyan-Armenian. But we're both filled
with the Spirit!

We're both reconciled to God! We're building a team and
it includes all kinds of churches coming and working together.

The next thing we're going to do and I want to announce
it in faith — I've been busy for the last year and a half working
on something God told me to do. He told me to build a new
community right in the heart of Washington, D.C., and when
those congressmen are driving to the hill, they can't miss it.
We're going to name it "Reconciliation Square." It will run
from N Street to New York Avenue and from New Jersey Avenue to Fifth Street.

At the present time, we only own two-thirds
of one block, but God has given me the whole two-and-a-half
to three blocks. I know He has because He told me so. We're
going to get it and one day we're going to have you come
from north and south and east and west to see "Reconciliation
Village." Whites and blacks, rich and poor, the weak and the
strong, the young and the old — all living together because
we are ambassadors for Christ.